A Lived Theology of Everyday Life

A Lived Theology of Everyday Life

Encountering God in Work, Play, and Culture

Michael W. DeLashmutt

 CASCADE *Books* · Eugene, Oregon

A LIVED THEOLOGY OF EVERYDAY LIFE
Encountering God in Work, Play, and Culture

Copyright © 2025 Michael W. DeLashmutt. All rights reserved. Except for brief quotations in critical publications or reviews, no part of this book may be reproduced in any manner without prior written permission from the publisher. Write: Permissions, Wipf and Stock Publishers, 199 W. 8th Ave., Suite 3, Eugene, OR 97401.

Cascade Books
An Imprint of Wipf and Stock Publishers
199 W. 8th Ave., Suite 3
Eugene, OR 97401

www.wipfandstock.com

PAPERBACK ISBN: 979-8-3852-2439-5
HARDCOVER ISBN: 979-8-3852-2440-1
EBOOK ISBN: 979-8-3852-2441-8

Cataloguing-in-Publication data:

Names: DeLashmutt, Michael W. [author].

Title: A lived theology of everyday life : encountering God in work, play, and culture / by Michael W. DeLashmutt.

Description: Eugene, OR: Cascade Books, 2025 | Includes bibliographical references.

Identifiers: ISBN 979-8-3852-2439-5 (paperback) | ISBN 979-8-3852-2440-1 (hardcover) | ISBN 979-8-3852-2441-8 (ebook)

Subjects: LCSH: Christianity and culture. | Work—Religious aspects—Christianity. | Leisure—Religious aspects—Christianity. | Sports—Religious aspects—Christianity. | Education, Higher—Religious aspects—Christianity.

Classification: BR115.C8 D453 2025 (paperback) | BR115.C8 (ebook)

VERSION NUMBER 09/15/25

Scripture quotations are from the New Revised Standard Version, Updated Edition, copyright © 2021 National Council of Churches of Christ in the United States of America. Used by permission. All rights reserved worldwide. Emphasis added to quotations.

To Julia,
the one who transforms everyday into the extraordinary.
I will love you always.

Contents

Abbreviations | ix
Acknowledgments | xi
Introduction: Theology and Everyday Life | 1

Section 1: Method
1 Method of Correlation | 9
2 Understanding the Everyday | 22
3 Thinking About Popular Culture | 36

Section 2: Locations of Meaning Making
4 Theology, Cultural Analysis, and Sport | 55
5 Formed Theology: Transformation Through Making | 69
6 Theology, Culture, and the Environment | 84

Section 3: Theology at Work and Play
7 A Theology of Work | 101
8 A Theology of Play | 117

Section 4: Everyday Theology in Institutional Life
9 A Theology of Administration | 133
10 A Theology of Leadership in Theological Education | 142

Conclusion: The Ordinary Sacred | 155
Bibliography | 159

Abbreviations

ATS   Association of Theological Schools
NIGTC New International Greek Testament Commentary
QR   *Quarterly Review*
WW   *Word and World*

Acknowledgments

THIS BOOK IS THE culmination of over twenty years of research, writing, teaching, and leadership in higher education in theology and religious studies. So many people have contributed to this work that it would be impossible to thank them all adequately. First and foremost, I want to thank Pastor Ron McClung, my lifelong friend and *anam cara*—a loving presence, wise guide, and constant source of support and encouragement. Ron has been one of the few companions who journeyed with me from spiritual brokenness to flourishing. Academically, I owe deep gratitude to Prof. James Wellman, who, during my time at Fuller Theological Seminary, encouraged me to grapple with my evolving sense of religious identity. At the University of Glasgow, Dean Jeff Keuss sparked in me a passion for French phenomenology (and Ashoka's butter chicken). Prof. David Jasper taught me to explore the furthest reaches of theological imagination, running boldly with ideas to unexpected corners. Dr. Michael Fuller, through the Scottish Episcopal Institute, played a formative role in my journey toward Anglican theology. To the Rev. Dr. Brannon and Gloria Hancock, your enduring friendship has been a steadfast source of strength. To Prof. Mike Higton, thank you for giving me my first academic position at the University of Exeter. To the Rev. Keith Lamdin, who exemplified what it means to be a faithful and courageous Christian leader, I am deeply grateful. I also wish to thank the Rev. Dr. Christian Scharen, who took a chance on "repatriating" this UK Yankee and welcomed me into theological education in the United States. Your belief in me and your guidance have meant

Acknowledgments

more than I can express. Over the past decade and a half of academic leadership, friendships have been a vital lifeline. Pastor Eric Samuelson and Dr. Ryan Torma, your constant support has given me the courage to lead—and, just as importantly, the wisdom to step away from leadership when necessary. For the past decade, my time at General Seminary has shaped me profoundly. I am deeply grateful to this community for all it has taught me and all it has offered my family. Serving at General has come with significant challenges, but I will always treasure the friendships—those I have lost and those I have retained—among the faculty, staff, and trustees. Through seasons of joy and extraordinary hardship, this community has shaped me. The "close community" that once flourished here continues to be a source of joy. I am particularly thankful to Shauna and Aaron Niequist, as well as Jonathan Merritt, for their encouragement to find and use my voice, which gave me the courage to publish this book, and to my friend and colleague Ian Markham who pushed me to "finish the damn thing."

Last, and most importantly, I am grateful to the extraordinary women of my family, particularly my mother, Jane, and two sisters, Alicia and Diana. You have shaped me into the person I am today, and your unwavering support and unconditional love have been constant gifts for which I am endlessly thankful.

Above all, Naomi and Eliza, being your father has been the most transformative experience of my life. You have taught me how to be a better human being. I am in awe of the incredible individuals you have become, in spite of having me as a parent!

In all these relationships and countless others—friendships and connections that have woven together the fabric of my everyday life—I have come to know the love of God. For this, I give thanks.

Dean Michael, The Feast Day of Florence Li-Tim Oi 2025

Introduction
Theology and Everyday Life

ONE OF THE QUESTIONS that perennially haunts me as a theology professor is this: "What difference does all this faith stuff make?" I mean, clearly, trusting in God, seeking to serve Christ in all persons, committing to regular practices of prayer and worship—all of this should do something. These practices ought to transform not just how I spend my Sunday mornings or Wednesday evenings but also how I live every moment—from extraordinary mountaintop experiences to the mundane details of everyday life.

In short, this is the task of this book: making sense of theology in everyday life. While this will all be explored in much greater detail in the chapters below, from the outset, I want to unpack a very cursory definition of how I'm using these three terms: sense making, theology, and everyday life throughout the rest of this book.

SENSE MAKING

By sense making, I mean something like "meaning" or "intelligibility." Now, it could be argued that starting a theological book with something as subjective as meaning may not be ideal. Shouldn't theology—and particularly Christian theology—begin with God rather than with human concerns? Of course, this is correct! Theology—along with all of creation—begins with God's action. The very fact that I am writing these words, and you are reading them, testifies to God's prior presence and action in the world. God

Introduction

does not need to be invoked or invited to be present; God is always and already here, active in the world.

Making sense of the activity and presence of God is one of the ways that we can learn to see and know better the God who is already at work in the world. Perhaps this practice of seeing and knowing will help us recover some of that enchantment that Max Weber suggested is lost with modernity or resist the exclusive humanism Charles Taylor describes in *A Secular Age*—the belief that nothing outside of our own human experiences or interests exists in the world. I hope that through this book we can explore ways to see, know, and make sense of God in the middle of our everyday lives.

THEOLOGY

There was a time when I thought of theology purely as an academic and intellectual pursuit. By the end of my seminary education and well into my doctoral research, I had grown distanced from a lived and ecclesially embedded faith. As a teenager in a Pentecostal church, I had experienced a deep love of Scripture, a fascination with the mysterious work of the Spirit, and the richness of Christian community. Yet I also experienced spiritual harm at the hands of poorly trained clergy who extinguished my adolescent faith through their actions and words.

Disillusioned, I left the church in my twenties, and while I no longer believed in or practiced the faith that had led me to seminary in the first place, I remained in graduate school—in part because I still found theology immensely fascinating and in part because I wanted to see if, behind all of these books and beliefs, there was any truth to be found. In my immediate post-church era, I was bitter, skeptical, and pretty sure that while theology was a great thing to study, the religion that sometimes emerges from theology (and the theologies that sometimes emerge from religion) were at best a mental exercise.

Today, former Evangelicals call a process like the one I went through twenty years ago "deconstruction"—a word I only recently understood exclusively in terms of postmodern philosophy of the sort one reads in Derrida. For slightly-younger-than-me post-Evangelicals, "deconstruction" means something like the process of remaking a particular kind of evangelical faith and replacing it, more often than not, with a kind of quasi-mystical progressive Christianity. For me, however, my critical approach to Christian theology led to the relative safety of the academy. I saved myself

Introduction

from having to ask the "what does it mean" type questions that I hope we will engage in this book by focusing more on the beauty of theological discourse—as a kind of spiritual and intellectual poetry that had little to do with how we actually lived our lives and certainly far less to do with any metaphysical commitments about the being or person of God.

As a young, skeptical academic, I was interested in learning more about so-called radical theologies and the idea of the death of God. I was attracted to the writings of Thomas Altizer, Don Cupitt, and John Robinson and other more "liberal" theologies that sought to make sense of the traditions of the church in light of the "modern world" (variously understood). The approaches that were most attractive to me allowed me to think about theology as a kind of "history of ideas" without needing to step into the messiness of being part of a faith community or wrestling with the idea of a personal and interventionist God. I hoped that by studying theology in a secular context, I could hold on to something like a cultural Christian humanism or Christian deism while supporting my fascination with the aesthetics, stories, histories, poetry, and legacy of Christianity—all the while keeping myself safely wrapped in a thoroughgoing materialist framework that had little space for the God of the Bible or the church.

It turns out that while I wasn't able at the time to believe in the God of the Bible or the God of the church, God was still at work in my life. (I still hear the opening two lines from The Script's hit "Breakeven" every time I think of this period of my life.[1]) Eventually, in my post-evangelical, Christian-humanist, secular, and deconstructing phase of life, I found myself standing around a stone altar in the university chapel of the University of Glasgow, just across the square from the Faculty of Divinity. There, an old Scottish Episcopal priest (who likely was then younger than I am now) led us through the strange (to me) words of the eucharistic liturgy. In the intimacy of this gathering of three or four university students (myself included), led by a priest dressed in clothes whose names I had yet to learn (cassock, alb, stole, and surplice), with the strong smell of port filling my nose in a way that matched how the sense of God's abundant love began to fill my heart, I felt myself transforming. I like to say that in these fifteen-minute Eucharists, I could believe in God again. The liturgy was for me (as I often tell my students today) a cast within which the broken bones of my soul began to heal. Liturgy, which for Anglicans is a living expression

---

1. Frampton et al., "Breakeven."

of theology, helped me to recover from the abuses foisted upon me in my youth and taught me how to be a Christian again.

I tell this story because it highlights something of the unique flavor of theology that I am hoping we can explore in this book. I believe that theology is God's radically gracious self-disclosure of God's character as love to humanity—even to a humanity that (like me) may not even believe in love, grace, or God in the first place. As the former presiding bishop of the Episcopal Church Michael Curry liked to say, "If it's not about love, it's not about God." While I tend to dislike sloganeering, I do think there's something to this one. As the earliest Christians wrote in 1 John 4, "God is love," and I believe that the study of theology is a way in which we come to know that source of love at the very center of the universe. It is, in short, how we learn to love God with our minds.

EVERYDAY LIFE

The final term is "everyday life"—sometimes referred to here as "the secular," "culture," or "the quotidian." By this, I mean what phenomenologists like Edmund Husserl call the "lifeworld": the constellation of places, memories, practices, histories, and events that shape our experience of the world. In this book, I'm especially interested in the mundane elements of the lifeworld—those aspects of life that might seem trivial or unrelated to faith but are, in fact, deeply infused with God's presence.

We will spend time thinking about God in connection with something as seemingly ephemeral as popular culture (film, TV, podcasts, and movies), sports (which has a fascinating religious history, even if it may not seem to be the case on the surface), and our actions toward and attitudes about the environment (since much of our current environmental crisis is actually a consequence of our consumerist cultural practices).

Lest we think that God is only part of the life that we live when we're off the clock, I also want to spend some time looking at how God is present in the complexities of work and institutional life. It seems to me, in a world where we are increasingly defined by what we do for a living (just think about how many times you find yourself asking a new person, "What do you do?" as a substitute for "Who are you?"), we must learn to look for how God might make God's self known to us within our working lives. Because cultural studies (one of the disciplines that we will employ throughout this book) gives preference to concrete examples drawn "from the ground" (in

Introduction

contrast to theories developed only in abstraction), I will use two case studies drawn from my own experiences in institutional leadership as a way of thinking through how I have made sense of theology amid my own working life, in order to encourage you to do the same in yours.

The God whom Christians love is the sort of God who appears in unexpected places. Not just on mountaintops or in burning bushes but in the mouths of shabby prophets or stubborn donkeys and from the pens (or keyboards) of sinners and saints who are captivated by a love that changes lives. This is a God found most clearly in the least likely of places, like in the womb of an unwed teenage girl from an unremarkable mountain village in first-century Galilee. In short, I am convinced that God is active, present, and disclosing something about God's self to us in all manner of places—at play and at work. This conviction undergirds the chapters that follow, which draw from diverse and often surprising elements of life—from popular culture and sport to the practices of making art, to leading higher education institutions and faithfully managing institutional change.

A BIT ABOUT THIS BOOK

This book is connected by the overarching theme of making sense of theology in everyday life. These questions have occupied me for most of my two-decade vocation as a theologian and educator. Some chapters, like those on sport or popular culture, were written years ago and reflect the context of their time. Others, like the chapters on theological education and the theology of making, are more recent. Though the topics are diverse, together they demonstrate the central thesis of this book: God is always present amid our everyday lives, inviting us to be found by God.

Section 1
Method

1

Method of Correlation

When I was very young, my father owned a John Deere tractor dealership in Malvern, Iowa. Mills County Equipment comprised a modest, white, corrugated metal-clad building (where my father's office and the parts counter were located) with a massive three-story tractor repair shop behind. It was prominently situated on a hill between the town's diminutive main street and the interstate off-ramp. Driving up the surprisingly steep driveway (steep for Iowa!), you were greeted by dozens of iconically green-painted tractors of varying sizes and shapes parked in concentric circles around the buildings.

Some of my favorite memories with my father were spent in or around John Deere tractors. While I was never allowed to drive them (as I was the baby of the family and a profoundly clumsy child, the privilege was reserved for my more competent middle sister), Dad often took the time to explain to me how the tractors worked. I loved the cutaway diagrams of the combine harvesters printed inside the sales brochures, which showed the complex process by which rows of corn were fed through the harvester, mechanically cut and shucked, with the grain sifted and stored in the grain bin behind the combine's cab, while the chaff was expelled out the back to be tilled back into the soil ahead of the next growing season.

These memories instilled in me an appreciation for understanding how things work, not only how they were used. This, I believe, is why I've always felt compelled to begin any course or written work with a section on method. The how and why of what we are about to embark on are, for me, as important as doing the thing itself.

Like learning how farm equipment works, I think it is important for us to understand how theology works within the context of everyday life. After all, the dilemma I mentioned in the introduction—the perennial question of what difference trusting in God makes to the mundane elements of life—reflects this concern. How does faith, which often seems conceptual or theoretical, make a difference to "the real world"? Conversely, in what way do our experiences and contexts in "the real world" shape what we believe and how we practice our faith?

THE METHOD OF CORRELATION

To begin this process of making sense of theology in everyday life, I want to advocate for a particular kind of theological method: the "method of correlation." This approach to theological meaning making, which gained traction among theologians in the mid-twentieth century, connects our experience of everyday human concerns with the deep world of meaning in Christian theology. Through this method, one seeks to demonstrate how the Christian faith can, with endurance and relevance, address us in the midst of our world today. Often, the method does not start with doctrinal formulations of faith directly but rather with the existential situations of human life, correlating these with the message of the Christian faith. In this way, it attempts to make theology relevant to contemporary life, showing how theology can speak directly to the conditions and questions of everyday existence.

Correlation, for the purpose of this book, should be distinguished from causation. Correlation implies a relationship between entities (e.g., first A, then B, then C), whereas causation implies causal effect (e.g., A causes B, which causes C). I'm highlighting this subtle distinction because it underscores how the relationship between theology and culture is not necessary in a technical sense. Simply put, culture could exist without theology, and theology could exist without culture—though the separation of the two is to the detriment of both.

This distinction is more than academic. The God we aim to know in this book is not a nebulous presence or force but a person (and, as a Trinitarian theologian, it would be more correct to say "persons"). As a person, God may choose to be present to us—or not. God is always free to show up where God wills and to be absent where God wills. There is nothing, other than God's own assurances or promises, that guarantees that God is or is not to be found in any given cultural form. My view is that we should seek neither in theology nor in culture to create idols in which the presence of the divine could be made present on demand. God is present to us in culture—or not—because God chooses to be present to us—or not—in a given form.

The method of correlation encourages us to discern and inquire about the presence (or absence) of God within a given context, rather than presuming that God's presence is guaranteed simply because something is religious or spiritual (e.g., sacred music) or necessarily absent because something appears secular or areligious (e.g., attending a sporting event).

BACKGROUND: HISTORY, CULTURE, SUSPICION, AND CORRELATION

Much of this chapter engages with the work of three pivotal figures in twentieth- and twenty-first-century cultural and correlational theologies: Paul Tillich, Graham Ward, and Kathryn Tanner. While correlational theologies and theologies of culture have been central concerns of recent generations of theologians, such theologians were by no means the first to engage in interdisciplinary theological inquiry that takes seriously other domains of knowledge and experience.

For example, Clement of Alexandria (150–215) made frequent use of Stoicism and Platonism in his writings; Origen (185–254) taught an explicitly Christianized form of Platonism; and Augustine used Neoplatonic thought among a panoply of other extant philosophies and religions in his own writing. Well beyond the patristic period, from the Middle Ages onward, Christian theologians continued to interpret the Christian message using extra-Christian sources. Thomas Aquinas (1225–74) extensively employed Aristotle to reframe Christian doctrine. Friedrich Schleiermacher (1768–1834) produced a theology consonant with Romantic philosophy. Paul Tillich's (1886–1965) thought was shaped by existentialism. Even Karl Barth's (1886–1968) *Church Dogmatics* had a highly contextualized understanding of the word of God. Those involved in shaping the Christian church have always articulated their theology in reference to—and in the shadow of—the thought forms, cultures, and imaginative frameworks of

Section 1: Method

their times and places. The building blocks of theology are rarely restricted to the authoritative sources inherent within the Christian church's canons.

In our present age, often termed the late-modern era—a period stretching perhaps from the mid-nineteenth century to the present—this interest in relating theology and culture (the task of a correlational theology) has become increasingly important. As noted by David Ford:

> Between the European Middle Ages and the end of the nineteenth century there were many major events and transformations of life and thought, often originating in Europe but with global consequences. Chief among these have been the Renaissance and Reformation, the Colonization of the Americas, the Enlightenment, the American and French Revolutions, the rise of nationalism, the Industrial Revolution, and the development of the natural sciences, technological medical science, and the human sciences. There has also been the combined impact of bureaucracies, constitutional democracy, new means of warfare and of communication, mass education and public health programs, and new movements in the arts and in philosophy and religion. Theologians have been members of societies, churches, and academic institutions through this innovative, traumatic period, and their theology has inevitably been influenced by it. That is how, in a minimal sense, their theology is modern: by taking account of such developments, even if sometimes in order to dismiss, criticize, resist or try to reverse them.[1]

Some suggest that the increased interest in contemporary culture stems from a tacit need on the part of Christian theologians to defend anew the veracity and sensibility of theological claims to truth and meaning. Questions related to the enduring meaning of Christian theological claims have been explored in greater detail by scholars with a particular interest in secularization and secularity. Charles Taylor's *A Secular Age* is perhaps the most significant of these. While the five-hundred-year journey from a Western world in which belief in God was largely taken for granted (at the start of the Reformation) to the twenty-first-century world in which belief in God is one of a range of possibilities—and often an option with diminishing plausibility—is worthy of deeper discussion, this chapter introduces three significant modern thinkers described by late twentieth-century philosopher Paul Ricoeur as "the three fathers of [the hermeneutics of] suspicion": Marx, Freud, and Nietzsche.[2]

---

1. Ford et al., *Modern Theologians*, 1.
2. Ricoeur, *Freud and Philosophy*, 33.

Karl Marx (1818–83) notoriously regarded religion as the "opiate of the people," viewing it as a paralyzing fantasy that, when abused by those in power, obscures the true nature of the human condition. Friedrich Nietzsche (1844–1900) recognized that the theological assumptions that once held together a common European culture were no longer plausible. Finally, Sigmund Freud (1856–1939) rejected religion as a misplaced fantasy or projection originating within the human mind. Following these critiques, a widespread statistical decline of religion in the West (primarily in Europe) has precipitated ongoing discussions of the so-called secularization thesis and the future of religion in the West.

In an age of suspicion—when the veracity, efficacy, and necessity of religion are in question—theologians are challenged to reconsider how theological meaning is constructed. As contemporary culture grows increasingly skeptical of traditional religion, the nature of God's relationship to the world comes under scrutiny. Is culture a genuine avenue through which we can encounter God, making it a potential medium of divine disclosure? Or does the culture of the world stand in opposition to the culture of the church, requiring critique or rejection by people of faith? Wrestling with these questions may not be optional; rather, it reflects a core task of theology in the modern era.

THEOLOGIANS OF CORRELATION

There are many theologians I could choose to engage with as I seek to articulate a theology of correlation, but I want to introduce three figures who have made an enduring impact on my own thinking. Paul Tillich was a renowned professor at Union Theological Seminary in New York City during a time when questions about the ongoing significance of God and the veracity of faith were hotly debated in mainline denominations like my own. While I don't always agree with Tillich's conclusions, his lasting impact on my corner of the Christian church has endured through decades. Graham Ward reflects another important stream of thought. Ward, an Anglican priest and theologian, has often been associated with the so-called radical orthodoxy school. While Tillich seeks to bring cultural questions into dialogue with theological language (we might say theology learns the dialect of culture), Ward is often associated with an approach that favors placing orthodox theological categories in a more prominent, authoritatively higher position in the dialogue. Finally, Kathryn Tanner—one of the greatest living Anglican theologians in the United States—has spent her career wrestling at the fringes of theology and other disciplines, pushing the boundaries of both culture and theology, allowing a prophetic critique of both to emerge from the dialogue.

The theologians discussed below grapple with the challenge of doing theology in a culture marked by suspicion. Their work often draws on history, politics, and the arts as they seek to understand how theology can speak meaningfully to the present. In this text, we describe these efforts to relate theology to culture as a theology of correlation, and to this topic we now turn.

DEVELOPING A METHOD OF CORRELATION

Paul Tillich

Paul Tillich (1886–1965) was a German-born theologian who lived and worked in both Europe and the United States. A prolific writer, Tillich's existential approach to Christian theology contributed greatly to developments in both liberal theology and practical theology throughout the twentieth century and into the present. Tillich argued that we can encounter the source of theology not only through the conventional sources of authority found in Scripture and tradition but also through human history and culture. The process of history and the expressions of that process through human culture shape and inform our theological understanding, providing a means by which humanity can authentically encounter God—or, in his language, "Ultimate Concern." The norms by which we judge whether cultural forms are authentic ways of encountering God stem from the content of the biblical message itself and are determined by the criteria of the doctrine of justification by faith, the incarnation of Christ as the New Being, the Protestant principle (the unceasing creative and critical power of authentic religion), and the cross of Christ (a symbol of God's negation and affirmation of human history).

In his later theological method, Tillich describes this approach of encountering and assessing Ultimate Concern through the language of the "method of correlation," which is the process by which the individual theological practitioner engages the deep, ultimate, or existential questions of the world with the answers provided by the Christian message.[3] There is

3. Tillich, *Systematic Theology*, 1:59–62.

an inherent tension in this view of correlation, which some describe as a dialogue between faith and culture, while others interpret it as a one-sided conversation in which the answers of the Christian faith address the questions that faith presupposes in the world. The reason Tillich's theology of correlation appears to privilege the position of the Christian theologian is that, for Tillich, the theologian always engages with the "other" (culture, philosophy, etc.) through what he calls the "theological circle." This circle symbolizes the in-faith-ness of the theologian, describing the presuppositions or faith commitments that theologians inevitably bring to any discussion or dialogue with culture.

The difference between Tillich's method of correlation—which sees the Christian message as an answer to the world's questions—and most other variations of this method lies in the extent to which these approaches privilege either the Christian presuppositions (the theological circle) or the questions posed by the world's situation. In the chapters ahead, as we consider various ways to engage in dialogue between theology and everyday life, it is useful to keep in mind the methodologies espoused by correlation theologies as they relate to the ongoing outworking of such dialogues.

Tillich's theology is also famous for its creative approach to theological language. While Tillich employs familiar words like "Christ," "Spirit," and "church," he frequently uses them in ways that differ from traditional usage. Though Tillich regarded theology as essential to the church's ongoing self-understanding, critics have argued that his ecclesiology was inadequately developed. As a corrective to what might be seen as Tillich's fuzzy ecclesiology, the Dutch Catholic theologian Edward Schillebeeckx developed a historical-critical theology that correlates the Christian message with what he identifies as universally and historically evidenced "constants" within human culture. Writing slightly after Tillich, Schillebeeckx understands correlation as the natural language of the church, which continually attempts to describe in Christian symbolism the objects of concern that preexist in the world. He writes:

> But although they [the world and the Church] are talking about the same thing, they are doing it from different points of view. That is why dialogue is necessary and why both the world and the Church, owing to the special contribution which each makes, need a two-sided conversation about their work for the welfare of men.[4]

---

4. Schillebeeckx, *God the Future*, 133.

Section 1: Method

If, for Tillich, theologians engage in correlation primarily to exercise a theological apologetic (addressing the questions of the world with the answers of the Christian message), for Schillebeeckx, the church engages in correlation to prophesy to the world. The church's ministry is "a role in which it is critical of society and at the same time socially utopian."[5] Thus, Schillebeeckx advocates for a new self-definition of the church's teaching office as the prophetic power of the church to critique and constructively dialogue with the world. For this prophecy to be effective, however, the church must listen to both divine revelation and the "foreign prophecy" spoken by the "secular situation."

I am reminded of the method of correlation almost every time I sit down to write a sermon. As a young preacher, fresh out of seminary, I was so captivated by the internal language, structure, and content of Christian theology that my sermons often became theology or history lectures. I neglected the task of bridging the gospel's meaning with the needs and situations of the gathered worshipers in my church. For me, theology had become the whole of my world. I ignored the possibility that (1) God might speak outside theology books, and (2) my job was not to teach my congregation the history and method of the incarnation but to explore how trusting in Jesus Christ, the fully human and fully divine One, might make a difference in raising a family, combating systemic racism, or finding hope in struggles with addiction or mental illness. This is not to say the method and theory of theology are unimportant; rather, it means that theology is shaped and unpacked by its context—whether in a pulpit, at a café, or on a bike ride. Theology becomes a conversation between tradition, the interpreter, and the present context of ministry and life.

FURTHER TAKES ON CORRELATION

Canadian Jesuit theologian Bernard Lonergan further developed the method of correlation by proposing a "transcendental method" that considers the individual theologian's role as a mediator between religion and culture. For Lonergan, the task of correlating theology with culture involves a kind of conversion—a mixing of horizons where both theology and culture are transformed through dialogue. This mutual change recognizes that theology itself evolves in engagement with new cultural contexts.

---

5. Schillebeeckx, *God the Future*, 136.

Not all theologians view this openness to cultural transformation as beneficial. Robert Doran, in *Theology and the Dialectics of History*, critiques correlation for relying on sources outside Scripture and the magisterium, fearing this undermines theology's foundation. Meanwhile, David Tracy contends that correlation does not go far enough in acknowledging the transformative potential of theology's encounter with culture. Tracy's method posits two principal poles for theology: Christian texts and common human experience and language. While Tillich correlated existential questions with Christian answers, Tracy argues for a "critical correlation" that evaluates both the situation and the message. For Tracy, theology and culture hold equal weight in dialogue, allowing theology to adapt fluidly to cultural changes.[6]

Roger Haight sought to reconcile these concerns, integrating ecclesial continuity with Tracy's openness to cultural change. Haight argues that all theology—received or emerging—is shaped by its context, both contemporary and historical. His *Dynamics of Theology* articulates a correlational theology where Christian symbols mediate encounters with the transcendent. For Haight, "The method of correlation is not a method of theology, but the method of a discipline that seeks to preserve the meaning of the past while understanding it in a distinctly present-day manner."[7]

Haight's iteration of correlational theology largely guides this project. However, since Haight is not the final word in theology and culture, we now turn to a brief overview of additional postmodern and contemporary voices.

Contemporary (Postmodern) Approaches to Theology and Culture: Tanner and Ward

Most of the approaches to theology and culture that have been discussed above originated within a context of modernist skepticism, inherited from Enlightenment rationality that was nurtured by a culture of scientific reason that aligned with the hermeneutics of suspicion. Yet what if these particularly modern ways of thinking about the world were no longer held to be universally valid? Some would argue that during the latter half of the twentieth century, the cultural and intellectual climate of modernism changed, and the door was opened to new ways of thinking about God, the world, the self, and human community. In what could be termed a

6. Tracy, *Blessed Rage for Order*.
7. Haight, *Dynamics of Theology*, 132.

"postmodern era," the position from which theologians and theological practitioners conceive of the relationship between theology and culture has shifted quite considerably. Rather than thinking of theology and culture as two examples of timeless and universal opposing points of view—and certainly rather than thinking of theology as the purveyor of an absolute truth—conceived within the world of postmodern thought, the theology and culture dialogue becomes far more particular in its scope and contextual in its application. Indeed, a project such as this text is a reflection of such a postmodern approach to theology and culture, insofar as we begin by putting theology and culture into dialogue within a common world (remember the axiom repeated above: culture shapes theology, and theology informs our encounter with culture). We are engaging not in some grand description of culture as either the whole of human creativity or the best of human creativity but rather in an exploration of particular forms of the texts and practices of everyday life.

This postmodern construal of theology's relationship to and in culture is found largely in the work of scholars who are engaging theology in the context of the broader discipline of cultural studies (a subject to be discussed at length in the following chapter). Though we will be engaging with a variety of theologians who are trying specifically to make sense of theology and popular culture (within the popular cultural areas of film, literature, media, music, etc.), at this point we should acknowledge the work of two theologians, Kathryn Tanner and Graham Ward, whose very different usage of culture marks a creative reimagining of the theologies of correlation and opens up the possibility of doing theology in wildly diverse cultural landscapes.

Kathryn Tanner

Like David Tracy, Kathryn Tanner is skeptical of the method of correlation. For Tanner, correlation theologies fail to attend to the concrete, historical, and particular natures of both Christian theology and the cultural situation. Neither culture nor theology exist in a vacuum; both are historical, contextual, and highly particular. By trying to sift through culture and theology to find common points of reference, correlation theologies have neglected to recognize that cultural and theological meaning are always arrived at through hermeneutics. Rather than focusing on how theology can answer the questions posed by culture (Tillich), Tanner encourages her reader to see theology as a tool that can be used for understanding and critiquing one's cultural context (thus orienting her project in a way that is not dissimilar to the "prophetic" form of correlation advocated by Schillebeeckx, above). However, we should be clear that Tanner's use of theology is always highly contextualized. She writes:

> One does not first determine a distinctively Christian message or lens for viewing the world and then bring it, subsequently, into relation with other cultural practices for, say, apologetic purposes; those other cultural practices are there from the beginning as the materials out of which the very Christian message or lens is constructed. . . . A kind of apologetics or polemics with other cultures is internal . . . to the very construction of Christian sense.[8]

Though the sentiment above wouldn't sound out of place in Haight's *Dynamics of Theology*, where Tanner shows her true theological ingenuity is in her appeal to twentieth-century cultural theory. Unlike Tillich, in particular, who uncritically employed the human sciences as a resource for "doing" theology, Tanner asserts that theology must be both aware of the influence exerted upon the theology of culture by theories of culture and—when appropriate—provide a critical voice that can influence such theories of culture. For example, whereas the modernist approach to cultural anthropology favored viewing cultures as geographically limited, unified, yet autonomous wholes that could directly influence human behavior, a postmodern approach to cultural theory recognizes the complex, global, and interconnected nature of culture. Such a postmodern view would emphasize how the individual member or subgroup within a culture both shapes and is shaped by the whole (asserting that the member of a culture is empowered to determine the nature of that culture). Furthermore, postmodern theories of culture give a privileged place to the practices of everyday life and assert that issues of meaning, value, and power are primarily negotiated "on the ground."

Therefore, Tanner considerably enlarges the resources that are made available to the theologian for thinking about how theology relates to culture. By encouraging theologians to make use of postmodern theories of culture, she opens up new ways for theologians to think about culture and gives us a mandate for attending to facets of everyday life (like our engagement in popular culture). Moreover, by reframing the theology of correlation as a relation of uses rather than a relation of form and content,

---

8. Tanner, *Theories of Culture*, 116.

she encourages theologians (as anticipated in the work of Schillebeeckx) to speak prophetically into the broader sphere of culture and cultural theory.

Graham Ward

For Graham Ward, theology's engagement with culture is more than just a matter of translating theological language into culturally intelligible language or drawing from the cultural imagination to better understand theological concern; the theological engagement with culture is fundamentally an exercise in political engagement and social transformation. To accomplish this politically minded project, Ward reminds his reader that in a postmodern context, theology and religion are necessarily public forms of discourse:

> Religion does not live in and of itself any more—it lives in commercial business, gothic and sci-fi fantasy, in health clubs, themed bars and architectural design, among happy-hour drinkers, tattooists, ecologists and cyberpunks. Religion has become a special effect, inseparably bound to an entertainment value.[9]

Like Tanner, Ward's theological project combines traditional theological sources of Scripture and tradition, with a strong grounding in cultural theory and postmodern philosophy. In order for theology to understand its context, it must rely on the methodologies and techniques of cultural studies and the social sciences. Such disciplines reliably tell us about the world and can provide insight into Christian truth. Yet not only does cultural acuity provide the theologian with a greater purchase on truth; becoming familiar with one's culture enables one to offer a theologically grounded cultural critique which speaks to the inadequacies of human culture. Concern with cultural critique is shot through Ward's growing body of work, especially in his *Cities of God*, which playfully addresses questions of corporality, identity, and hope in the postmodern city; through *Cultural Transformation and Religious Practice*; and most recently in his *Politics of Discipleship*, which offers the clearest picture to date of Ward's theo-political project aimed at creating a "Christian theological imaginary that might modify and transform aspects of that civic imaginary that is so antithetical to Christian living today."[10]

---

9. Ward, *True Religion*, 132–33.
10. Ward, *Politics of Discipleship*, 17.

CONCLUSION

In Tanner and Ward, and indeed in their twentieth-century predecessors in the theology of correlation, we find an attempt within the context of modern or postmodern thought to rearticulate the Christian message in a way that is both intelligible (by using the language of our modern or postmodern world) and applicable (by attending to the situation of that world). Indeed, one could argue that theological language is always striving to be spoken in a way that speaks to a particular people, whether in the time of the writing of the stories of Genesis during the Babylonian exile of the sixth century BCE, in the proclamation of the Christian message in the early centuries of the church's history, or in the current era in which we find ourselves today.

We've seen in this chapter that theology can be a porous dialogue partner, one that learns from other disciplines, context, and practices. Theology provides a frame of reference for reading and interpreting "everyday life" and also is itself reread, reinterpreted, and applied in different ways, depending on one's own cultural context.

If theology and culture are always and already in some form of a dialogue, then it makes sense that we must also seek to understand the cultural context that we find ourselves in. To help us with this, in the next two chapters we are going to learn how to "read" culture, first through an introduction to cultural studies and second by looking at some specific examples of how and why theologians and theological practitioners engage with popular culture.

2

Understanding the Everyday

In 2002, my wife and I quit our jobs, sold our home and cars in a western suburb of Seattle, and packed all our earthly belongings into four very large suitcases. We moved to Glasgow, Scotland, so I could pursue a PhD. Living in Glasgow, I became keenly aware of the truth behind the old saying that Britain and the United States are two countries separated by a common language. Among the various English dialects, Glaswegian must be one of the most challenging for a North American ear to comprehend.

Our flat on White Street, just off Byres Road, was situated above an older couple who were likely in their seventies and who had lived in the same apartment since "the war." Passing by them in the common hallway, my wife and I would attempt polite small talk. Despite many months of light and friendly banter, I am fairly certain we understood only two or three sentences exchanged between us in total. For all I knew, their "Happy Christmas" could just as easily have been a complaint about my noisy footfalls or the smell of my cooking.

After about a year, our ears began to adjust to the Glaswegian dialect. The uniquely Gaelic words, idiomatic phrases, and thick pronunciations slowly started making sense. Before long, we could sit in a pub with friends and understand the majority of what was being said. However, being understood was a different matter entirely! For our part, we had to shift how we spoke as well. On the phone, I described our apartment number (3/B) as "three-stroke-B" instead of the American "three-dash-B" to convey that we lived on the third floor in flat B. When ordering a small latte at Starbucks (a rare treat that reminded me of our former home near Seattle), I'd ask for the "wee" size rather than the "short." Casual greetings transformed into "Hiya," and goodbyes into "Cheery-bye," replacing my usual "Hey, what's up?" or "Later."

My academic and professional writing changed too. I added *u* to words like "color" and "flavor," swapped the *er* and *re* in words like "center" and "theater," and embraced the distinctly Scottish antonym for "within"—"outwith." These adjustments, alongside countless other small shifts, altered my listening, writing, vocabulary, and speech. I adapted in all these ways to better navigate and engage with a (only slightly) different cultural and linguistic context.

Culture operates similarly. It comprises the mundane, often unnoticed, fabric of daily life: the casual greetings exchanged with a cashier, the small talk at a crowded pub, or the rituals we follow without reflection. Culture isn't something we always attend to, and stepping outside of it often provides the first opportunity to recognize its contours. It's like asking the proverbial question: "Does a fish know it's wet?" Culture surrounds us completely, but seeing it clearly requires adopting a stance of attentiveness.

INTRODUCTION TO CULTURAL STUDIES

The work of developing a stance of attentiveness to culture is the aim of the discipline of cultural studies. Raymond Williams (1921–88), one of the field's early pioneers, famously remarked that *culture* was "one of the two or three most complicated words in the English language."[1] For Williams, culture is not simply the preserve of the wealthy, a norm dictated by elites, or the products of distant civilizations (all of which are alternative definitions of the term). Rather, he insisted, culture encompasses the everyday: "Culture is ordinary, in every society and in every mind."[2]

This understanding of culture aligns with one of the approaches we will take in this book, though it is by no means the only way to define such a slippery term. As we will see, our modern understanding of culture has evolved significantly over the past 150 years. This evolution includes the culture and civilization tradition, which regarded culture as "the best which has been thought and said"; Marxist readings of culture, developed by the Frankfurt School, which framed culture as a vast system of production and

1. R. Williams, *Keywords*, 87.
2. R. Williams, *Resources of Hope*, 3.

Section 1: Method

consumption; and more recent postmodern approaches, which highlight the creative agency of cultural consumers and the ways they derive meaning from existing cultural forms.

In the sections that follow, we will briefly explore how culture and popular culture have been understood and studied over the past century and a half by focusing on key figures and themes. As noted in the previous chapter's discussion of Tanner's *Theories of Culture*, an era's theology of culture is often shaped by that era's theories of culture. Reflecting on these cultural theories can help us better identify the implicit assumptions that inform our own theological engagement with culture. Moreover, as encouraged by the examples of Tanner and Ward in the previous chapter, becoming familiar with emerging trends in popular cultural theory equips us to offer our own theologies as unique, creative, and empowering rereadings of contemporary culture.

This chapter begins with an overview of how culture was understood prior to the rise of cultural studies, specifically through the culture and civilization tradition and Marxist readings of culture. From there, we will discuss major trends within the disciplines of cultural studies and popular cultural studies. This exploration will reveal a consistent tension in the study of culture, one that juxtaposes cultural expression with ideological, political, and economic concerns. As we examine these theories and movements, it will be useful to keep three questions in mind:

- Origins: How does this theory describe the origins of culture? Does culture emerge organically from within human communities (from below), or is it something created by one group to be consumed by another? Who determines what constitutes "good" or "bad" culture?

- Ideologies: In what ways is culture used as a means of control? Is culture deployed by the state or other forces to exert their will on the masses, or does it possess subversive and liberating potential?

- Economies: To what extent is culture shaped by market forces? Does the mass production of culture diminish its aesthetic authenticity? Which takes precedence: the artistry of culture or its economics?

On the surface, culture may seem fleeting, trivial, or insignificant. In reality, however, our engagement with culture—as consumers, producers, and critical thinkers—implicates us in a vast and complex system. This system is where creative, economic, and political values intersect and vie for dominance.

Understanding the Everyday

THE CULTURE AND CIVILIZATION TRADITION

Imagine living through the late Industrial Revolution in nineteenth-century Britain. To sustain the relentless demand of industrialized cities, the English countryside was drained of both its workforce and its identity. Northern cities expanded at a staggering pace as the children of farmers, miners, and bakers abandoned ancestral trades to labor in factories. These rapidly growing urban centers lacked the social ties and cultural practices that once defined village life. In their place, workers and their families endured unimaginably harsh conditions, living in rows of terraced houses. Entire households, including children, worked grueling shifts, often exceeding twelve hours, performing repetitive tasks with little time for rest, education, or the development of cultural or aesthetic sensibilities.

The urban working classes, shaped by these new realities, developed a cultural identity distinct from the preferences of the elite minority. For social reformers and educationalists like Thomas Arnold (1795–1842) and his son Matthew Arnold (1822–88), this working-class culture was viewed with suspicion and fear. To them, working-class neighborhoods appeared chaotic, lawless, and rife with poverty and disease. A proposed solution to this perceived disorder was a campaign of cultural reform.

In the 1830s, Thomas Arnold argued in letters and pamphlets that the church bore a responsibility to improve the conditions of the working poor. This mission included building new churches and schools, as well as promoting lay-led ministries within impoverished urban areas. By serving the poor within their own contexts, the church could preserve the population's moral and spiritual character, while countering the chaos of urban life.

Matthew Arnold retained his father's zeal for reform but shifted the focus. For him, the responsibility for cultural uplift extended beyond the church to the educated elite. In his seminal *Culture and Anarchy* (1869), he framed the duty of cultured elites as a divine calling to bring "the best that has been thought and said in the world" to the working classes, ensuring that "reason and the will of God prevail." He writes:

> The whole scope of the essay is to recommend culture as the great help out of our present difficulties; culture being a pursuit of our total perfection by means of getting to know, on all the matters which most concern us, the best which has been thought and said in the world, and through this knowledge, turning a stream of fresh and free thought upon our stock notions and habits, which we are now following staunchly but mechanically, vainly imagining that

there is a virtue in following them staunchly which makes up for the mischief of following them mechanically . . . the culture we recommend is, above all, an inward operation.³

This vision underpinned much of the socially oriented work of the Church of England in the nineteenth century. The construction of Anglican churches in industrialized London and the booming cities of the North, the Romantic aesthetic of emerging worship styles, and the Pugin-inspired redecoration of parish churches across England all aimed to bring "culture and civilization" to the poor, uneducated, and alienated lower classes.⁴

The influence of this tradition extended into the mid-twentieth century, most notably in the work of F. R. and Q. D. Leavis. While the Leavises were primarily concerned with the state of English literature, their critique of popular and mass-produced culture—particularly the popular novel— echoed the Arnoldian emphasis on cultivating aesthetic sensibility. Q. D. Leavis, dismayed by the literary standards of mass-produced English fiction, famously predicted that such works would lead to the extinction of literature and the death of the novel. For the Leavises, mass culture weakened aesthetic sensibilities, which could be corrected only by the "severer self-discipline" practiced by the properly cultured.⁵

Classical Music Makes Your Baby Smarter!

The culture and civilization tradition sought to promote social harmony by offering victims of industrialization opportunities to appreciate "the best that has been thought and said in the world." This ethos persists in contemporary arts education projects, where governments fund free public access to art museums or provide classical music instruction to disadvantaged students. It also surfaces in consumer products like Baby Einstein, marketed to parents as a way to boost their child's intelligence by exposing them to the music of Bach and Beethoven—even in utero.

While these initiatives are often laudable, the culture and civilization tradition fundamentally frames culture and education as tools for

---

3. Arnold, *Culture and Anarchy*, 199.

4. The Arnoldian zeal to promote social reform through spiritual, educational, and aesthetic enlightenment was further reflected in the Reform Act (1867), which led to significant improvements in education, political representation, military service, and healthcare (Connell, *Influence of Matthew Arnold*, 157).

5. Leavis, *Fiction and Reading Public*, 225.

maintaining systems of power that favor the values and vision of a ruling minority over a largely disempowered majority. As *Culture and Anarchy* implies, culture was imagined as a means of staving off social disorder. Again and again, we see culture associated with ideology: it is used—whether intentionally or not—to reinforce, challenge, or subvert particular worldviews.

This tradition assumes that culture must be intentionally cultivated and developed, rather than something that arises organically from human practice. While elites may view their cultural promotion efforts as beneficial, this approach often neglects—or even disparages—the cultural expressions of the "masses."

As we turn to examples of Marxist readings of culture, we will see these concerns amplified. Marxist theorists shift focus from the social upheaval of industrialization to the cultural products facilitated by modern industry. Their critiques center on the mass production and consumption of cultural goods and the role these processes play in manipulating "passive" audiences.

In the early twentieth century, as industrial techniques were applied to the creation and distribution of cultural forms (mass-produced fiction, music, cinema, and reproductions of fine art), debates about the role of culture in society took on new urgency. The next section explores these debates and examines the interplay of economy and ideology within the context of popular culture.

MASS CULTURE THEORY AND CULTURE INDUSTRY

While Leavisites argued that the damage caused by mass culture was primarily aesthetic, another approach to popular culture studies suggested that the ideological and economic frameworks shaping our engagement with popular culture have a deeper and more systemic impact on society than mere harm to aesthetics. The Frankfurt School—an interdisciplinary group of social theorists including Theodor Adorno, Max Horkheimer, Ernst Bloch, Walter Benjamin, Wilhelm Reich, Erich Fromm, Herbert Marcuse, Wolfgang Fritz Haug, and Jürgen Habermas—sought to uncover the systems of power embedded in culture that exert control over unsuspecting masses. They contended that history is best understood as a narrative of development, with each historical epoch defined by its particular "mode of production." Consequently, a society's economic practices—its

Section 1: Method

patterns of production and consumption—determine its social, political, and cultural realities. For the Frankfurt School, cultural objects and practices could be comprehended only within the context of their specific historical circumstances.

For Theodor Adorno and Max Horkheimer, the products of the "culture industry" were cultural goods designed to be predictable, unchallenging, and easy to consume. Popular fiction, jazz music, and cheaply reproduced works of fine art were seen as artifacts manufactured by the culture industry. These cultural products served to reinforce political and economic control by offering a false sense of stability and security to those ensnared by capitalism. Adorno and Horkheimer argued that nations with successful socialist revolutions lacked the prevalence of mass culture that persisted in capitalist societies. In their view, mass culture hindered revolutionary change in capitalist democracies by shaping desires and providing artificial means to satisfy them, thereby preventing the emergence of a revolutionary consciousness rooted in authentic liberation.

Authentic culture, in this framework, challenges its audience to engage critically and constructively with society rather than merely entertains. The culture industry, as Marcuse observed, diminishes "the antagonism between culture and social reality through the obliteration of the oppositional, alien, and transcendent elements in the higher culture by virtue of which it constitutes another dimension of reality."[6] Here, "higher culture" becomes synonymous with "authentic culture," and the escape from mass culture requires the creation of an alternative cultural framework rather than altering how we engage with mass culture.

Both the culture and civilization tradition and the Frankfurt School share a common suspicion of the cultural activities associated with the working classes. In both approaches, the cultural tastes of the masses are deemed inferior to those of the elites—either refined by exposure to high culture or liberated from capitalist systems through a commitment to socialist ideals. However, what mechanism can reliably assess whether the cultural preferences of one group are superior to another? Moreover, within the seemingly homogeneous realm of mass culture, might there not be significant variations between subgroups or localities? Finally, is it accurate to assume that participants in mass culture are passive consumers devoid of agency in their consumption habits? One of the Frankfurt School's significant limitations

---

6. Marcuse, *One-Dimensional Man*, 58.

was its dismissive view of the working class's "taste" and its underestimation of their capacity to produce meaningful culture.

Recovering Agency in Culture

The previous section highlights a stark juxtaposition: an established "higher" culture that aims to educate or liberate versus a more organic "lower" culture that entertains, corrupts, or pacifies the masses. While this assessment will be challenged in later sections, particularly those addressing popular culture, it reveals an important recognition: culture is not confined to "the best that has been thought or said," but is instead a constellation of meaningful texts and practices produced, consumed, and creatively reinterpreted by groups regardless of their position in a hierarchical class system.

This recognition, that culture transcends class and aesthetic hierarchies, is foundational to the discipline of popular culture studies. Popular culture studies open avenues for the kind of engagement between theology and everyday life that constitutes the broader focus of this book. By paying disciplined attention to the "stuff of everyday life," popular culture studies expose the limitations of earlier approaches that reduced participants in mass culture to passive subjects controlled by either cultural elites or the industries producing cultural goods. While popular culture is clearly more than mere production and consumption, it remains deeply embedded within political and economic structures. To fully understand our engagement with popular culture, we must analyze it within concrete historical realities.

Political economic theory, particularly the concept of hegemony, offers a valuable framework for such analysis. Hegemony, frequently associated with the work of Italian Marxist philosopher Antonio Gramsci, describes how dominant groups maintain cultural and ideological control by securing the "spontaneous consent" of subordinate groups. Within the context of mass culture, hegemony operates not through coercion but by aligning with the reasons and desires of the working classes, who voluntarily engage with popular culture.[7]

Hegemony reorients our understanding of popular culture away from an isolated focus on production and consumption systems toward a nuanced analysis of how consumers exercise agency through acts of consumption. This shift, emblematic of popular cultural studies, prioritizes the will and actions of the consumer over the intentions of producers and distributors.

---

7. Storey, *Introduction to Cultural Theory*, 226.

Section 1: Method

In contemporary cultural studies, Angela McRobbie revisits the centrality of ideology and hegemony. Drawing on neo-Gramscian theory, she critiques the naive celebration of consumerism as the primary mode of meaning making in postmodern culture. Instead, McRobbie situates consumption practices within broader political and social structures, framing them as acts of "reproduction." She advocates for deep ethnographic studies of culture, focusing on the lived experiences that animate popular culture. This approach extends Gramscian cultural analysis, emphasizing the interplay between everyday life and structural power dynamics in shaping culture.[8]

STUDYING CULTURE, AFTER CULTURAL STUDIES: POSTMODERNISM AND POPULAR CULTURE

According to Richard Hoggart (1918–2014), founder of the University of Birmingham's Centre for Contemporary Cultural Studies, cultural studies is a social scientific discipline that seeks to analyze and critically evaluate cultural forms to understand their relationships to political economy. As a social scientific discipline, it applies a variety of quantitative and qualitative research methods to the study of cultural forms and practices. Underlying this approach is the belief that the elements that make up the superstructure (the cultural world) both shape and are shaped by the foundational systems describing the formal organization of society (political and economic realities).

In our media-saturated twenty-first-century context, it may not seem revolutionary to argue that we can gain unique insights into how our world is organized and run by attending to cultural forms like television, film, and music. However, for Hoggart and his successors at the University of Birmingham, focusing on the cultural world—particularly the popular cultural worlds of everyday life—represented a revolutionary step. This marked a departure from the speculative discourse on culture that characterized the modernist anthropological study of culture, which had been dominant for the previous one hundred years. This new approach moved away from abstract speculation toward a more practical understanding of political economy through cultural analysis.

Though the study of popular culture was always a facet of cultural studies (as seen in the work of Roland Barthes and Umberto Eco, who analyzed aspects of Western popular culture ranging from advertising to

8. McRobbie, *Postmodernism and Popular Culture*, 27.

popular fiction), popular culture studies emerged as its own academic subdiscipline in the 1980s. It combined cultural studies and communication studies, aiming to understand how artifacts from everyday life explicate political and economic realities. Additionally, popular culture studies showed an early interest in questions of value, class, and taste that were implicit in cultural consumption.

The theological study of popular culture is a relatively recent development, stemming from the intellectual traditions of cultural studies, communication studies, and popular culture studies, with the added contribution of theology. While practitioners of theological studies of popular culture may not always recognize their indebtedness to these disciplines, many of the topics raised by the theorists discussed in this chapter have influenced theological perspectives on culture, as we will explore in chapter 3.

HERMENEUTICS OF POPULAR CULTURE

Semiotics, Structuralism, and Post-Structuralism

The preceding approaches to studying culture share a common concern for the impact of mass or popular culture on the stability of the state, the aesthetic standards of an elite class, or the welfare of the working classes. However, as we turn toward more hermeneutic readings of popular culture (and, by extension, the study of everyday life), we encounter a more playful approach to interpreting cultural texts and practices. Political and economic concerns still loom large, but the methods become more dynamic. The first hermeneutic approaches we examine are structuralism and post-structuralism.

Structuralism, rooted in the work of Swiss linguist Ferdinand de Saussure, influenced a wide array of disciplines, including Marxist theory (Louis Althusser), literary and cultural criticism (Roland Barthes), philosophy and history (Michel Foucault), psychoanalysis (Jacques Lacan), and anthropology (Claude Lévi-Strauss). Saussure's major contribution to structuralism was the differentiation between language as communication (*parole*—speech and writing) and structural language (*langue*—a system of signs governed by rules).

Building on Saussure, Belgian social anthropologist Claude Lévi-Strauss applied this framework to the analysis of culture and myth. He argued that myths convey a similar dual schema: the structures of myth represent universal characteristics of the human mind, while the communication of myths is observed in the stories and cultural signs themselves. Structural analysis of myths, Lévi-Strauss contended, reveals deep truths common to all humanity, obscured by the surface-level variations of mythic expression. Applying this analysis to culture demonstrates how underlying structures of meaning can reduce diverse linguistic, artistic, legal, and religious forms to universal human experiences.[9] Structuralism thus provides a means of interpreting popular culture and everyday life as revealing universal human truths accessible only through skilled cultural critique. Famously, Lévi-Strauss's technique was applied by Italian structuralist Umberto Eco to analyze Ian Fleming's James Bond novels.[10] This approach demonstrated how cultural artifacts could reveal deep-seated structures underlying seemingly trivial narratives.

While structuralism seeks to uncover the meanings embedded within language (Saussure) or mythology (Lévi-Strauss), cultural semiotics uncovers the meanings behind specific cultural objects and practices. Roland Barthes's *Mythologies* (1957) exemplifies this approach, analyzing myths embedded in advertisements, magazines, dining, and sports. Barthes demonstrated how everyday cultural objects perpetuate bourgeois ideals, suggesting that processes of signification lie just beneath the surface of our engagement with the cultural world.

Post-structuralism challenges the foundational premises of structuralism. Post-structuralists argue against Saussure's assertion that texts contain fixed, inherent meanings. Instead, they posit that meaning arises through the interaction between text and reader, shaped by specific contexts and evolving over time. Prominent post-structuralists like Michel Foucault, Jacques Derrida, and Julia Kristeva emphasize the instability and multiplicity of meanings. Derrida's concept of "deconstruction" reveals contradictions and instabilities within texts, while Foucault's work on discourse and power demonstrates how language and knowledge interweave with power structures, shaping interpretation. Post-structuralism thus shifts focus from universal truths to the dynamic, context-dependent processes of meaning making, offering nuanced interpretations of popular culture as contested and negotiated.

---

9. Lévi-Strauss, *Structural Anthropology*, 21.
10. Eco, *Role of the Reader*.

Psychoanalysis

Psychoanalysis examines the origins and intentions behind human behavior and thought. Founded by Austrian neurologist Sigmund Freud, psychoanalysis proposes the existence of unconscious mental processes that influence conscious actions. Freud's interest in interpreting dreams—a practice he saw as analogous to interpreting cultural texts—has been particularly influential.

A psychoanalytic reading of popular culture can adopt either an author-centered or reader-centered approach. The author-centered perspective treats cultural texts as the equivalent of an author's dreams, interpreting subconscious motives and latent meanings. Freud's essay "Delusion and Dream [in Jensen's *Gradiva*]" (1907) explores this method, suggesting that texts can reveal the subconscious workings of their authors' minds.

In contrast, the reader-centered approach examines how texts guide the fantasies of their audiences. For Freud, texts provide a "fore-pleasure," setting the stage for imaginative engagement akin to dreaming. Laura Mulvey's seminal essay "Visual Pleasure and Narrative Cinema" exemplifies this method. Mulvey critiques the "male gaze" in cinema, arguing that films often subordinate women to serve the neurotic needs of the male ego. Her psychoanalytic methodology deconstructs patriarchal unconscious structures, advocating for cinema that liberates women from objectification.[11]

In contemporary discourse, Slavoj Žižek represents a dynamic psychoanalytic approach to popular culture. Drawing on Hegel, Marx, and Lacan, Žižek's work creatively interprets cultural texts to uncover insights about fantasy, reality, desire, and materiality. His *Pervert's Guide to Cinema* exemplifies this approach, using psychoanalysis to critique films and explore their cultural implications. While psychoanalysis offers insights, it remains inherently subjective, as interpretations depend on the associations the interpreter brings to the text.

Baudrillard: Popular Culture and Reality

Earlier in this book, we described popular culture as an ever-present background in everyday life. Jean Baudrillard's concept of hyperreality complicates this view, suggesting that popular culture does not merely reflect reality but constitutes reality itself. In *Simulacra and Simulation*, Baudrillard

---

11. Mulvey, *Visual Pleasure.*

examines the collapse of distinctions between reality and representation in a media-saturated age. He argues that simulations (copies without originals) generate the "hyperreal" where reality is indistinguishable from its representations.

This phenomenon shapes cultural practices and perceptions. For example, purchasing a branded item like a Gap shirt serves less to fulfill practical needs and more to perpetuate corporate branding. Similarly, technology like Apple's iPod integrates consumption with broader systems of economic and cultural reproduction. Baudrillard's insights reveal how deeply intertwined reality and popular culture have become, making theological engagement with the hyperreal essential.

CONCLUSION

"Culture" is a term that both distinguishes and unites. It is a word that has been appropriated to describe almost every facet of human life. In our twenty-first-century Western context, the culture that is commonly experienced as "popular culture" is the consequence of radical historical shifts in how humans produce and consume goods, engage in meaningful social interactions, and gather to form communities. Though past generations have been skeptical of the moral, social, or political values of popular culture, trends in contemporary scholarship highlight the importance of popular culture as a unifying ether in which we share a common frame of reference in an otherwise disconnected and fragmented world, as well as a resource for creative and constructive meaning making.

When Arnold and his fellow Victorian churchmen looked at the heaving slums of industrial Britain, they saw within them an anarchic mess that seemed in need of God's redemptive love. Today, when Christians look at the cultural context of the postmodern world, are we likewise inclined to assume that what our postindustrial chaos is in need of is redemption through the imposition of order, class, and culture, or are we able to approach culture and apply a more Augustinian approach, which seeks to understand the correlation between enjoyment of culture and the love for God?

In the following chapter, we will examine how this history of cultural criticism has influenced the attitudes toward and theories regarding mass or popular culture in the theological study of culture. It is important for theologians to (1) understand the complexity and scope of popular culture and (2) become at least casually familiar with the theories related to the study of popular culture. Understanding the complexity of popular culture helps one to be able to speak with some specificity about the nature of popular culture and to avoid excessive generalization. Popular culture is always historically and socially rooted. Perhaps even more so in our own time of bespoke podcasting, blogging, and user-generated content, one's experience of popular culture (in keeping with postmodern sentiment) is always very much a particular event. Moreover, becoming familiar with what others have said about popular culture enables theologians and scholars of religion to identify useful perspectives and resources for their own theological study of popular culture, the subject of the chapter to come.

3

Thinking About Popular Culture

THOUGH THEOLOGY (OR RELIGION) and culture have been paired together as topics for exploration and scrutiny since well before Matthew Arnold's *Culture and Anarchy* (1869), H. Richard Niebuhr's *Christ and Culture* (1950), or Paul Tillich's *Theology of Culture* (1959), approaches to theology and culture from the nineteenth century to the latter half of the twentieth century have gravitated toward two biases that are not particularly helpful for our present discussion. In general terms, such approaches have either centered on the relationship between theology and high culture (arguing that certain sorts of culture are particularly effective at achieving certain sorts of theological ends) or implicitly adopted what Kathryn Tanner describes as both a modernist and an anthropological approach to studying culture.[1] In regard to this latter point, this has meant a tendency to study culture from the "outside" and (especially in the case of theological studies) a neglect of the cultural embedding of the scholar. For those interested in a serious engagement with popular culture, either of these tendencies will prove problematic.

As an alternative to the assumptions that underpinned previous approaches to the study of culture, the emergence of cultural studies as a legitimate academic discipline in the 1960s both changed the way in which culture was theoretically understood and deepened the methodological resources for studying culture. Beginning with the work of Richard Hoggart, E. P. Thompson, Raymond Williams, and later Stuart Hall (all of whom

---

1. Tanner, *Theories of Culture*.

were associated with the Centre for Contemporary Cultural Studies at the University of Birmingham), cultural studies offered a renewed theoretical framework for understanding cultures. Cultural studies differed from more established approaches to studying culture that were gleaned from either cultural anthropology or Marxist readings of culture (such as those associated with the Frankfurt School). These scholars, and those who would come after them, gave special consideration to how the various practices, beliefs, institutions, and political and economic structures of a culture (as influenced by issues of class, ideology, gender, ethnicity, nationality, and sexuality) shaped the construction and distribution of meaning within a culture.

Parallel to the growth of cultural studies in the English-speaking world, the study of everyday culture has also occupied an important position in twentieth-century Continental thought. In particular, one could note Roland Barthes's *Mythologies* (1957), which applies semiotic theories to cultural texts as varied as advertisements for washing powder and popular fashion magazines; Michel de Certeau's *The Practice of Everyday Life* (1984), which discusses the strategies or tactics that one employs in the process of meaning making in a highly consumerist culture; or the various academic and popular works of Slavoj Žižek, which use Lacanian psychoanalysis to read the deep meanings present within the texts and practices at the margins of popular culture. These parallel trends in the academic study of the everyday life have provided dialogue partners, theoretical frameworks, and an impetus for much of the ongoing work in the theological and religious studies approaches to engaging with popular culture.[2]

One element of what distinguishes work being done today in the field of theology and popular culture from earlier attempts at studying theology and culture (as such), is the extent to which contemporary authors are squarely situating the subject matter of theology within their own experience of the complex interrelationship between the meaning-bearing texts and the meaning-making practices that make up everyday life.[3] Out of this experience, scholars are giving evidence to at least one of three assumptions about the relationship between theology and/or religion and popular culture: First, there is the belief that some degree of knowledge about God

---

2. For a fuller exploration of the history of both cultural studies and popular cultural studies, see Storey, *Introduction to Cultural Theory*.

3. A good example of this in the theological study of popular culture can be noted in the work of Tom Beaudoin (especially *Witness to Dispossession*), which effectively uses autobiographical theological reflection as a means of engaging with popular culture, among other issues.

Section 1: Method

(or religion) can be gained through a considered reflection on everyday life. Second (and related to the first) is the belief that God can choose to reveal Godself through any of a variety of cultural texts, objects, or practices. Third, there is a belief that studying popular culture is best done from the inside, thus making the study of theology and popular culture partially an exercise in what practical theologians refer to as "theological reflection."[4]

WHY I STUDY POPULAR CULTURE

Like many people who work in this field, my interest in theology and popular culture began as a way to bring together two seemingly divergent parts of my life: my involvement as a participant in—or consumer of—popular culture and my growing interest in a critical and creative reflection on my Christian faith, which took the form of an interest in Christian theology. For me, the process of making sense of theology and popular culture was not straightforward. The church tradition that I was part of during my early twenties was remarkably conservative. As inheritors of the American holiness-Pentecostal tradition, we didn't drink or smoke, we shied away from cinema (unless it was rated PG or below), and we listened exclusively to Christian contemporary music. There was a bawdy (or bawdy for us) joke that was frequently told about people who went to my conservative Christian university. It was said that on our college campus we didn't allow premarital sex because sex could lead to dancing! If a cultural form or practice was secular, we avoided it like a spiritual plague.

In the mid-1990s, I was a pastor at a small, nondenominational charismatic church near Seattle. It was the evening of the Fourth of July, and my wife and I were at a BBQ at the house of a parishioner. The parishioner's small bungalow had an exceptional view of our town's harbor, where later in the evening the annual fireworks display would begin. The mood was light and cheery, and in addition to the sounds of the bonfire crackling in the background and children running around playing, a nearby radio was tuned to a local pop-music station on which Joan Osborne's "One of Us" was softly but recognizably playing. In light of our avoidance of all things secular, it was unusual to hear a mainstream song playing on a mainstream radio station at a social gathering of our church friends (though, of course, the fact that I could recognize this pop song shows that my strict devotion to this form of cultural conservatism was already fraying at the edges).

4. E. Graham et al., *Theological Reflection*.

As I listened to the lyrics of this unremarkable pop song, something in me switched on. I was amazed to hear such a theologically important question about the nature of God's relationship to humanity discussed with such honesty and directness in the context of (of all places!) secular music. I found Osborne's lyrics to be a compelling indictment of the contemporary Christian culture I was so uncritically consuming at the time. In Osborne, I found someone from outside of "the church'" who was asking the kind of deep questions about the nature of God's relationship to the world in her trite pop music that I would have expected (though frequently didn't find) in the trite songs broadcast on the local Christian radio station. It shocked me that "out there in the world" one could find matters relating to God being discussed in deeper, messier, and perhaps more authentic ways than what I could frequently find in the Christian cultural ghetto within which my church and I were situated. Encountering discourse about God outside of the church started me on a journey to look for God "out there in the world." I wanted to know if there were other forms of culture that raised similarly deep questions about faith and to see if in culture itself there might be a way in which the knowledge of God could be found. It turns out that by looking for God in literature, cinema, music, art, and all manner of "secular culture," I have learned far more about love, beauty, value, community, and indeed, God, than I would have ever done by turning my back on the world.

In this chapter, I will outline some of the ways in which theologians and scholars of religion are today attempting to make sense of, with, and through popular culture. I'll begin by offering four examples of how we define popular culture and then move into a discussion of four basic trends that are prevalent among the work being done in the study of theology and/or religion and popular culture. Finally, I'll conclude by describing my own threefold approach to understanding theology and popular culture, as grounded in my experience of teaching the subject to students in the United States and the United Kingdom. Though this is hardly an exhaustive survey of the contemporary state of this emerging theological subdiscipline, as you read this, you'll gain a sense of where you can move forward in your own work in this field.

Section 1: Method

A POPULARITY CONTEST

I've been teaching on theology and popular culture for several years, and one of the initial questions that students ask me when encountering this subject for the first time is "How do we know what makes up popular culture?" We may, for example, have an intuitive sense that the music of Taylor Swift is popular culture and that a performance of Bach's *Goldberg Variations* is something different, but such tacit knowledge alone does not explain why we make such a distinction. Our assumptions are further complicated by how perceptions of cultural goods change over time. What happens to our arbitrary differentiation between popular and other kinds of culture when the music of Taylor Swift no longer serves as the soundtrack to our lives? Moreover, what if Bach's *Goldberg Variations* becomes popular when it is featured in the soundtrack of a Hollywood film or becomes the object of celebrity endorsements? When we talk about "popular" culture, we must be precise about how we are using this adjective ("popular") to modify its noun ("culture"). To help us clarify our language, let me suggest four potential meanings of "popular" in popular culture: quantitative, accessible, populous, and oppositional.

Quantitative

First, we could say that something is popular if it has wide appeal. Popular culture could be identified by looking at the Billboard Hot 100 charts for music, a newspaper's listing of the top-selling fiction books in a given week, or a list of the top-grossing films of a particular year. Though popularity is easy to determine using such metrics, the problem with the quantitative approach is that it ignores those elements of popular culture that may not be blockbusters yet nonetheless share a popular cultural aesthetic. For example, I am a fan of the Scottish band Belle and Sebastian, whose intentionally playful sound has earned them the genre label of "twee-pop." Though they play in a popular style, their fan base is relatively small, and their music has infrequently been at the top of the charts. So although the band is certainly a part of popular culture in terms of style, genre, and aesthetic, if we applied a strictly quantitative approach to defining popular culture, we'd have to rule them out.

Accessible

If the quantitative approach fails to convince us, we could choose to call something popular if it enjoys wide availability. In this sense, popular culture is that which the majority of the population has access to. Though I am nearly persuaded by this definition, again, it places perhaps too much emphasis on only those forms of popular culture that the majority of people can (or would want to) consume. As with the quantitative approach, defining popular culture by availability marginalizes those aspects of popular culture that may be slightly less commercially successful. Moreover, defining the scope of "wide availability" in a multinational context is not at all straightforward. Is something part of popular culture only when it is available for global consumption? If this is the case, we could consider the music of Michael Jackson as part of popular culture (in addition to online retailers, there's hardly a brick-and-mortar record shop in the world that wouldn't be able to sell at least some of his music), but what about the status of something that is fashionably popular in one location and not the other? In Britain, I have been struck by the popularity of news quiz shows like *Mock the Week* or *Have I Got News for You*, but such genres have no meaningful correlate in American popular culture. In America, country-and-western music is extremely popular, and you can find a wide selection of country-and-western radio stations all over the country. Yet in the UK, country and western is rarely broadcast on popular radio. Are quiz shows and country music not part of popular culture because their popularity is limited to particular national contexts? Clearly, we need to consider the local as well as the global if we use availability as a means of defining popular culture.

Populous

Third, we could define "popular" as originating from the people (as in the sense of something being populous). This view is distinct from those above, in that the way we arrive at our definition is informed by the creation of a cultural good rather than exclusively the consumption of that good. Along these lines, something is popular culture when we can say that it emerges from the work of the people (akin to what is frequently described as "folk culture"). However, though we could look at podcasts, flash mobs, independent music, and film as potential examples of populous popular culture, most of the cultural goods that we consume are actually produced through vastly complex processes. Whether we think of television programs, film, music, or consumer goods, rarely are popular cultural objects created by identifiable individuals or groups. If popular cultural goods and practices must be restricted to only those objects that can be traced back to a particular author, we'll find ourselves engaging with a very sparsely populated popular cultural world.

Oppositional

If we have found the meaning of "popular" in popular culture evasive, perhaps we could attempt to define popular culture by identifying what it is not. This oppositional approach tends to differentiate between authentic and inauthentic cultural forms as they relate to their origins or use among certain social classes (e.g., high, folk, and low culture). In the UK, for example, we could talk about the difference between the "popular press" (*The Sun* and *The Mirror*) and the "quality press" (*The Times* and *The Guardian*), or more generally, we could talk about the difference between popular cinema (like those associated with the Marvel Universe) and more serious cinema (like the films that air at the Tribeca Film Festival). Though intuitively, this may appear like a natural way of delimiting "popular" (or perhaps disposable) and "quality" (or perhaps enduring) culture, there are a number of problems with this view. Most importantly, differentiating between authentic and inauthentic cultural forms relies on a number of unspoken and unidentified class and value statements that one may unwittingly utilize when distinguishing between cultural forms. Indeed, rather than strictly analyzing culture, in so doing we may actually be imposing our cultural prejudices upon those individuals who consume particular cultural goods.

If a firm definition of the "popular" in popular culture escapes our grasp, perhaps we can identify some common themes from the four definitions advanced above. I would argue that despite their many differences, the quantitative, accessible, populous, and oppositional approaches all share a common theme that will prove useful in our ongoing discussion of popular culture in this chapter. I would suggest that "popular" is used in the four examples above to denote a space within our common life where there exists both the interchange between the consumption, production, and application of artifacts and the emergence of a context for shared corporate practices. Seen in this way, the study of popular culture (including artifacts and practices) is ultimately a way of uncovering and identifying our varied participation in the process of meaning making. Though we must take seriously the "stuff" that populates the cultural world, our goal when studying popular culture is not simply to develop a deeper appreciation of cultural forms but to seek a clearer understanding of the meanings that emerge through our engagement with popular culture.

Though the study of popular culture can be casual or fun, it also represents very important work. Popular culture is the place in which the big issues of our day can be expressed, explored, or satirized. We see in popular culture representations of our greatest hopes for ourselves and our society, as well as images that depict our deepest fears and anxieties. To be sure, some popular cultural texts and practices provide more fruitful resources for such reflections than others. But even things as apparently trivial as an episode of *Love Island* or the pop music of Ice Spice can provoke us with important insights into pressing cultural concerns. For theologians who are interested in understanding the way in which the gospel is interpreted or enacted in our present day, we cannot afford to ignore the important role played by popular culture in shaping our contemporary imaginative frame of reference.

THE TURN TOWARD POPULAR CULTURE

For the past twenty-five years, theologians and scholars of religion have given tremendous attention to the texts and practices associated with popular culture. During this time, the international professional organization for religion scholars, the American Academy of Religion, has run countless panels on "Religion and Popular Culture," along with sessions dedicated to studying the interplay between religion and new media, religion and film, and religion and music. Additionally, several professional research networks and organizations have been formed that encourage dialogue between theologians, scholars of religion, and cultural scholars (the Theology, Religion and Popular Culture Network is chief among these in Europe). Additionally, there are several online and offline journals (*Journal of Religion and Popular Culture, Journal of Religion and Film, Cultural Encounters*) that specialize in issues raised by the study of religion and culture and that provide an important forum for developing scholarship in the field.

This turn to popular culture among academics reflects a widespread belief that popular culture is an important locus for meaning making within the West. For scholars of religion, it implies that the way in which

Section 1: Method

popular cultural texts are used reveals something important about how people construct their sense of identity and purpose in a context that is described by many sociologists of religion as being "post-Christian" or largely secularized. In this environment, it is argued that popular culture forms a way in which individuals and communities interpret their shared and private experiences and, perhaps, experience the transcendent. For other scholars of religion, popular culture texts themselves have a strong and fascinating affinity with religion. Though they may not be explicitly used for religious ends, a critical reading of cultural texts and practices reveals tacit religious symbols that are at play within the cultural world.[5] Theologians have a related interest in how the texts of popular culture are both received and created; however, a theological approach to popular culture is largely concerned with how popular cultural forms challenge or change preexisting theological beliefs and practices.

There are many ways in which one could propose to examine the relationship between theology and/or religion and popular culture. Here, I wish to begin by walking through the approach noted by Bruce Forbes and Jeff Mahan in their edited volume *Religion and Popular Culture in America* and conclude by reflecting on my own threefold approach, which has been informed primarily by my experience teaching theology and popular culture in the context of formal theological education.

Forbes and Mahan identified what they saw as four prominent trends, which are reflected in the current work that deals with religion and popular culture: (1) religion *in* popular culture; (2) popular culture *in* religion; (3) popular culture *as* religion; (4) religion and popular culture in dialogue. According to the first approach, religion *in* popular culture examines the role played by religious themes within cultural texts and practices. One

---

5. There are perhaps too many contemporary texts dealing with the interplay between theology/religious studies and popular culture to list them all in this context. However, an excellent example of the approach noted here is Chidester, *Authentic Fakes*. Chidester argues that there is something deeply spiritual and religious within American popular culture. Though it is often hidden deeply beneath the surface, religious symbols and myths appear in everything from baseball to Disney and tell us as much about the role of explicit religious practice in America as they do about the profound importance of popular cultural forms in shaping tacit religious practices. Whereas Chidester is looking at cultural forms themselves, one could also look at the reception of cultural forms as a contributing factor in constructing individual and social identity and value. Such an approach is taken in Clark, *From Angels to Aliens*, which is perhaps one of the greatest examples of a ethnographic study dealing with the quasi-religious role played by popular culture in American society.

could think of the religious themes in popular music (like Lil Nas X's "Call Me by Your Name," Lady GaGa's "Judas," or Madonna's "Like a Virgin"), films (the religious orders depicted in Villeneuve's *Dune*, the complex interweaving of free will and fate in Nolan's *Tenet*, the important function of the priest in Clint Eastwood's *Gran Torino*, or the religious symbolism of the *Matrix* trilogy), and fiction (questions of human identity in an age of AI in Ishiguro's *Klara and the Sun*, the role played by faith in Yann Martel's *Life of Pi* or in Dan Brown's *Da Vinci Code*). Using this approach, religiously minded cultural scholars (or culturally minded religion scholars) can identify how religious themes are interpreted within contemporary culture and can identify the continued role played by religion in shaping our cultural imagination.

In their second approach, the study of popular culture *in* religion, Forbes and Mahan note how religious groups make use of cultural forms in order to effectively adapt their religious beliefs and practices to their surrounding cultural context. An example of this could be the hugely popular *Left Behind* series of Christian fiction, or the multimillion-dollar Christian contemporary music industry, which now extends to commodified worship music of the sort once associated with Hillsong. In both of these cases, the normative influence of what is largely an evangelical Christian faith has led to the creation of cultural goods that utilize the *forms* of popular culture as a way of expressing and underlying religious content.

In describing popular culture *as* religion (the third approach), Forbes and Mahan touch upon the body of work that describes how popular culture can serve a function in contemporary society that was once largely the purview of traditional religions. Popular culture, according to many scholars, takes on such a religious function when it is used as a means of creating communities, serves as a hermeneutic lens through which one could interpret the world, provides a set of meaningful practices, or perhaps gives participants a sense of something larger than themselves. We could see examples of this in esports and competitive gaming communities (e.g., League of Legends World Championship) where communities foster a sense of belonging and shared identity, similar to religious congregations; in the fandom surrounding the Marvel Cinematic Universe (MCU), in which, through MCU's expansive narrative and devoted fan base, a shared mythos and community are created, which echo elements of religious storytelling and fellowship; or K-pop fandom, particularly BTS ARMY, with its intense devotion and community activities among BTS fans that mirror religious practices of communal worship and shared purpose.

Finally Forbes and Mann suggest "popular culture and religion in dialogue" as something of a catch-all category for those examples of religion and popular culture that don't neatly fit into the other three categories. One could find here examples of the dynamic interchange between popular culture and religion, where religion is neither necessarily the subject of cultural creations (the first approach) nor the content of cultural objects and practices (the second and third approaches) but rather a site for creative religious meaning making within the context of popular cultural production and consumption. We could think of podcasts that discuss faith and culture, like *The Bible for Normal People*, which engages contemporary cultural issues through a theological lens; TV series like the *The Good Place*, which teach viewers all about moral philosophy and the afterlife in humorous yet profound ways; and perhaps crossover cultural forms like Nadia Bolz-Weber's *Shameless: A Sexual Reformation*, which engages with contemporary cultural issues around sexuality and faith. According to Gordon Lynch's fourfold typology, this is the place where "popular cultural texts and practices" are used as a "medium for theological reflection."[6]

Teaching Theology and Popular Culture

As noted above, religious scholars and theologians work very closely with one another in this field, and it is difficult, at times, to distinguish what is "theological" as opposed to "religious" about such analyses of popular culture. In what remains of this chapter, I want to offer a somewhat autobiographical reflection on a few lessons that I have learned as both a theologian and a theological practitioner (that is, the kind of person who tries to work out the practices of theology in the life of faith and ministry) while doing work with theology with popular culture. As I seek to articulate what a distinctively theological approach to popular culture is, I have found it useful to learn from the attitudes that have emerged from my interactions with students, during the few years that I have been teaching theology and popular culture in secular and religious universities, with theological courses, colleges, and seminaries in traditional and adult-education contexts in the UK and the US. As I will describe below, I see three approaches in the theological study of popular culture (which I'll refer to as the moral,

6. Lynch, *Theology and Popular Culture*, 21.

missional, and theological reflection approaches), that correspond to three types of students whom I will call the Marketer, the Curate, and the Disaffected Churchgoer.

The Marketer

For some time, I have been teaching an introductory course on theology and popular culture that has served as an elective or optional module at a number of different institutions. Because students are seldom required to take the course, I make a habit of asking students why they've signed up to study theology and pop culture in the first place. Among the expected answers ("I like the idea of watching films in class"; "I don't know much about popular culture and I think I should learn something"; "It worked out well with my schedule"), on one such occasion I received an answer from a student that has stuck with me for the past five years: "I signed up to Theology and Popular Culture because I think it will help me to be a more effective marketer in my ministry." In chasing up this answer I found that this student had cannily created a bespoke ministry preparation program at his American Christian university by combining courses from the university's new business school program with more conventional ministry courses (leadership, theology, pastoral counseling, and my elective in theology and popular culture), to help prepare himself to more effectively apply the lessons of the church growth movement with a modicum of cultural sensitivity.

The Marketer wanted to use the theological study of culture as a tool that would enable him to effectively communicate a theological message in an attractive and intelligible way as was possible. In so using culture as a missional tool, the Marketer's theological and moral sensibilities controlled the terms of the relationship. If a cultural form offended or challenged those sensibilities it needed to be sanitized or avoided. For example, in his classwork he was very excited to think about how social networking sites like Facebook or MySpace could be used as a way of extending his church's ministry or to learn about how principles drawn from advertising and marketing could produce more effective forms of church publicity. However, when he and his classmates were asked to engage with music that had explicit lyrics or fiction and film that might have had some sexual content, the Marketer would refuse to engage with these materials beyond what his moral sensibilities would allow.

Section 1: Method

The Curate

Before reflecting in more detail about the Marketer's moral approach to theology and popular culture, let's contrast the Marketer (an American university adult learner) with a person we'll call the Curate, whom I taught in an undergraduate ministry training course in the UK. Teaching about popular culture as an American expat in the UK, particularly to students who were often decades older than me, posed unique challenges. My UK teaching experience was primarily in adult education, with students preparing for public Christian ministry or returning to higher education for a new focus. These students ranged from their mid-thirties to mid-eighties. It is challenging enough to discuss popular culture with eighteen- to twenty-four-year-olds who might share a common understanding, but defining popular culture becomes even more complex when it spans generations and cultural icons from Tony Bennett to Terry Wogan, *Bonanza* to Bono.

When I would ask these students why it was that they were studying theology and popular culture, without fail they would talk about their desire to understand what exactly popular culture *was*; many had a sense that it was important, but most couldn't quite articulate why this was the case. When pressed further, students would describe how they wanted to be able to talk about their faith in a way that made sense in the context of contemporary culture (not unlike, I suppose, the marketing approach noted above), or they would say that they wanted to be able to use film clips or music or television as a way of initiating conversations about religious topics, or they would say that they felt that in order for their Christian faith to be relevant to those around them, they needed to understand their own missional context.

Though on the surface this missional approach to popular culture may seem to unite the Marketer and the Curate, across their different church traditions, their different nationalities, and their different demographics, there is a difference in their general orientation to culture. Whereas the Marketer is content to fix his gaze on the surface appearance of culture, the Curate is prepared to enter into a conversation with culture on issues of some depth. The difference between the UK midlife Curate and the young US Marketer is best expressed through one of my favorite teaching anecdotes.

Since it was released in cinemas, I've been using the 2006 Alejandro González Iñárritu film *Babel* in a variety of teaching contexts as a way of getting students to think theologically about film. I have been surprised by the different ways in which my UK and US students have responded to the film. While some of the students in the Marketer's cohort found the film to be very compelling viewing, the vast majority were unable to recognize any redemptive quality in the film because of its infrequent profanity and scenes of a mild sexual nature. In fact, so upset were several of the students that they made a formal complaint to the dean about my showing the film on a module in the university's school of ministry. In contrast, when showing the film to my UK Curates, nearly all of the students have been moved by the film and offered some very robust theological reflections stemming from the film (on topics like the weak depiction of women, questions of international justice, the theme of interconnectedness, etc.).

Although both Marketers and Curates were coming to popular culture in order to achieve a missional objective, they can be distinguished from each other by the degree to which they operated a generous reading of culture or allowed the cultural form to speak on its own terms. This is not to say that in either case it is possible or preferable to bracket out religious presuppositions. If Ricoeur's hermeneutics teaches us anything, it's that our reading of texts is always mediated through complex detours, of which religious faith is an example. Unlike the Marketer, the Curate was able to maintain a dialogue where faith informed culture and culture informed faith. In the case of *Babel*, the Marketer's concern for sexual purity, informed by his interpretation of Jesus' teaching about lust and adultery, made it impossible for him to watch the film in a way that opened him up to any redemptive or transformative encounter with the film's narrative. The Curate was able to watch the film and think about the theological message conveyed by the film (in terms of social justice, the nature of familial love, care of neighbor) but also to offer a theological critique of the film stemming from her strong reaction against the depiction of gun violence. Indeed, in every screening of the film in the UK, students have consistently focused on the ethical problems of gun violence as depicted by the film—a topic never once identified by my American students.

Disaffected Churchgoers

I want to conclude by describing a third type of student with whom I've worked on issues in theology and popular culture. While in my experience teaching in the context of accredited (that is, degree-leading) education, my students have largely been thinking about theology and popular culture with particular ministerial concerns in mind, when working in

Section 1: Method

nonaccredited lifelong learning environments, I have found students use popular culture largely as a way of expressing their inner spiritual journey. This was especially the case with those who felt that their spiritual or intellectual needs are no longer being addressed by their home congregations. In one such course on popular culture and spirituality, a group of these disaffected churchgoers described how traditional Christian theology, the creeds, prayer, and the liturgy had gradually, over time, stopped making sense to them and (in many cases) to their adult children. In response to this, I asked students to bring with them a video clip, a song, a passage from a novel, or another cultural object that they had found spiritually nourishing. These students, many of them clergy, found a language that spoke to their deep spiritual needs in popular cultural forms—whether the *Twilight* series of novels, films like *Gran Torino* or *About a Boy*, or pop/folk music like that produced by Mumford and Sons. These students, who shared a sense of disaffection from traditional Christian symbols, felt isolated from their received understanding of faith, religion, or God but were able to find a common language to express their spiritual sensibilities by appealing to popular culture as a source of theological reflection or as a site in which God was able to authentically disclose Godself to them.

The Marketer, the Curate, and the Disaffected Churchgoer demonstrated three different motives for engaging with popular culture, which could otherwise be described as a moral, a missional, and a theological reflection approach. For the *moral* approach to popular culture, how we engage with culture is determined largely by our moral and theological frameworks. Culture is regarded as distinct from, or even subordinate to, the moral universe of Christian theology. Though culture may be appropriated for missional purposes, popular culture must be scrutinized in order to prevent the moral contamination of the individual Christian by cultural goods. In the *missional* approach, though Christian theology still largely controls the terms of the relationship between theology and culture, the guiding concern is less private morality than it is public mission. If culture can aid in the effective promotion of the Christian gospel, the missional approach would encourage the church to be emboldened to use culture in whatever way is most effective. In the approach which I am referring to as *theological reflection*,[7] popular culture and theology are given even footing

---

7. I am indebted here to Gordon Lynch's fourfold typology: "1) the study of religion in relation to the environment, resources, and practices of everyday life; 2) the study of the ways in which popular culture may serve religious function in contemporary society;

and are allowed to interpret one another as dialogue partners. In this way, we allow culture to first speak to us, in its own language, before we seek to scrutinize culture for its missional worth or moral risk. Through such a relationship to culture, we are leaving open the possibility that God may choose to reveal Godself (or not!) through the texts and practices of our cultural world. Through the theological reflection approach, by remaining open to God's self-disclosure in popular culture, we may discover something about God that perhaps we might not have already known![8]

CONCLUSION

Given the increased pace at which books are being written and new courses are being taught, it appears to me that this particular theological sub-discipline is addressing a deep concern held by many of our readers and students (and perhaps also our colleagues). Like them, I feel the intense disparity between the imaginative frame of reference that is populated by our popular cultural world and the imaginative frame of reference populated by Scripture and tradition. By studying popular culture as theologians and theological practitioners, we are invited into the dynamic and transformative work of inculturation. This theological concept describes the process by which the Christian message and way of life are expressed authentically within a particular cultural context. More than simply adopting cultural forms, inculturation seeks to embed the gospel in such a way that it not only resonates with cultural elements but also serves as a force that animates, shapes, and transforms the culture itself. The ultimate goal of inculturation is to foster a mutual encounter where both the gospel and the culture are renewed and enriched, leading to the realization of what theologians have described as "a new creation."

Inculturation builds on the belief that God's revelation is both universal and particular, capable of being expressed within the language, symbols,

---

3) a missiological response to popular culture; 4) the use of popular cultural texts and practices as a medium for theological reflection" (*Theology and Popular Culture*, 21).

8. As David Bosch has noted, "The early Christians did not simply express in Greek thought what they already knew [about Jesus Christ]; rather they discovered through Greek religious and philosophical insights, what had been revealed to them. The doctrines of the Trinity and of the divinity of Christ . . . for example, would not be what they are today if the church had not reassessed itself and its doctrines in the light of the new historical, cultural situations during the third through the sixth centuries" (*Transforming Mission*, 190).

and practices of any given culture. This process allows the gospel to become incarnate in diverse contexts while maintaining its integrity. Rooted in the church's missionary mandate, inculturation draws from scriptural precedents, such as Paul's approach to the Athenians in Acts 17, where Paul proclaims Christ using the philosophical and religious language of his audience. Similarly, theologians today are called to discern how popular culture—whether through music, film, art, or digital media—can serve as a site for theological reflection and proclamation.

As Pope John Paul II emphasized, the work of inculturation requires a careful balance: "The process of inculturation is thus a profound and all-embracing one, that involves the entire life of the Church and the whole of her missionary effort."[9] In engaging with popular culture, theologians can both affirm the ways it reflects human creativity and critique the ways it falls short of divine purposes, ultimately seeking to renew culture in light of the gospel.

---

9. For further discussions on inculturation, see Paul VI, *Evangelii Nuntiandi*, §§20–21. Also see John Paul II, *Redemptoris Missio*, §§52–54. For a broader theological framework, see Bevans, *Models of Contextual Theology*, which provides a helpful exploration of inculturation as one model of contextual theology.

Section 2
Locations of Meaning Making

4

Theology, Cultural Analysis, and Sport

> Heavenly Father, Divine Goalie.... Help us stay within the blue line of Your commandments and the red line of Your grace. Protect us from being injured by the puck of pride. May we be ever delivered from the high stick of dishonesty.... May You always be the Divine Center of our team and when our summons come for eternal retirement to the heavenly grandstand, may we find You ready to give us the everlasting bonus of a permanent seat in Your coliseum. Finally, grant us the courage to skate without tripping, to run without icing, and to score the goal that really counts—the one that makes each of us a winner, a champion, an All-Star in the hectic Hockey Game of Life. Amen.[1]

MUCH OF THIS BOOK stems from my experience of teaching theology—often interdisciplinary theology, like theology and popular culture—in a variety of settings. Teaching these courses, exploring how faith and everyday life intersect, has been a source of personal and spiritual transformation for me. It has grounded my relationship with God and deepened my trust in God's saving love for the world within the context of daily life.

While there are countless examples of God "showing up" in unexpected places—whether in a moving lyric, a beautiful painting, or a challenging film—there are also places where faith and culture collide in ways

---

1. Invocation of Father Edward Rapp before the 1976 World Hockey Association All-Star Game; as quoted in Prebish, *Religion and Sport*, 53.

that demand a more nuanced approach. Surprisingly, one such intersection is the relationship between theology and sports.

Students often have mixed reactions to my mention of sports in a theological classroom. Some are uninterested and may tune out, while sports fans might be skeptical of critiques that question the morality of sports or suggest that sports function as a quasi-religious phenomenon. For those finding this chapter tough going, rest assured: I am not a sporty person. My friends often tease me about my lack of sporting knowledge. I'm the type who watches the Super Bowl for the commercials and halftime show. Uncoordinated and without a background in playing or watching sports, I may seem like the last person who should write this chapter!

Yet, this chapter is not written by a sports fan for other sports fans. Instead, it explores the historical and sociological links between theology and sports, seeking to understand their relationship in light of contemporary popular culture. We'll discuss gladiatorial events in ancient Rome alongside something you might watch on ESPN.

This exploration will proceed on three levels. First, we'll examine the historical relationship between Christianity and sports, constructing a moral case against sports based on the writings of the third-century church father Tertullian of Carthage. Though Tertullian witnessed the bloodlust incited by arena events and viewed them as incompatible with Christian virtues, more recent church history tells a different story.

Second, we'll consider the missiological case for Christian engagement in sports, focusing on the twentieth-century legacy of muscular Christianity. This movement conflated physical fitness and hardy outdoorsmanship with spiritual virtues, leading to innovations like "sanctanasiums" and even shifting church service times to accommodate major sporting events.

Finally, we'll analyze sporting events themselves as objects of theological reflection. Sociologists often note the "religion-like" power of sports, drawing parallels between sports fandom and religious devotion. If sports function as a kind of religion, what values do they impart to people of faith? How can sports be understood theologically?

A NOVICE IN THE ARENA

As noted above, my exposure to sports is limited. Yet, I did once attend a professional American football game several years ago while living in Seattle, Washington, and that game left a significant impression on me!

Walking into the massive sixty-thousand-seat Qwest Field, where the Seattle Seahawks played, I was struck by the energy of the place. People exhibited uncharacteristic levels of outward emotion, wore elaborate costumes or body paint, drank overpriced microbrews, and abandoned their normal behaviors for this shared event.

I thought to myself, "Right, I'm an academic. I will treat this experience with critical detachment. Perhaps I can observe something useful for a book someday." I had read accounts linking religious-like devotion to sports attendance and wanted to witness this phenomenon firsthand. Yet, despite my standoffish intentions, I was quickly drawn into the event. By the second half of the game, I had spilled my third $12 beer and screamed myself hoarse cheering for the players on the field.

The only other time I had so thoroughly lost myself in the energy of a group was during revival services as a Pentecostal teenager (albeit without the beer and body paint!). The power of sporting events to evoke feelings and behaviors from individuals—compelling them to transcend their day-to-day existence, mobilize around a shared purpose, and forge collective identities—provides ample reason for theologians to reflect on the relationship between sports culture and faith.

A CASE AGAINST SPORT

Tertullian (AD 160–220) was a church father from the North African Roman city of Carthage. Born to pagan parents, he trained for a career in law but, after his conversion to Christianity in his thirties, dedicated his life to the service of the church. Tertullian was both an important theologian—the first Christian writer to use the term "Trinity" to describe the relationship between the three divine persons—and an apologist who defended Christianity against public slander. Later in his life, Tertullian joined a Christian sect known as the Montanists, which emphasized moral purity and chastity of the will. The Montanists were eventually deemed heretical due to their high view of ongoing prophetic work by the Spirit and their non-Chalcedonian Christology.

Despite this historical complexity, Tertullian is still regarded as one of the most influential writers from the late second and early third centuries. Indeed, it is from Tertullian that we have such memorable quotes as "What has Athens to do with Jerusalem?" (denoting the superiority of revelation over reason) and "The blood of martyrs is the seed of the church" (denoting the centrality of sacrifice in Christian life).

As an apologist, Tertullian wrote to defend Christianity against a wide range of slanderous claims made about Christians throughout the empire. These included allegations of atheism (the church's Christocentric monotheism was misconstrued as a denial of all gods), cannibalism (Christians were accused of eating the flesh and drinking the blood of their founder during the Eucharist), and sexual impropriety (Christians were accused of engaging in orgies and incest during their communal gatherings).

While these allegations certainly impacted the church's ability to thrive, it was not so much this litany of alleged practices that impeded Christian flourishing but rather the antisocial orientation these practices represented. What most directly contributed to the church's persecution was its stubborn inability to fit into the rhythm of life within the Roman Empire. Christianity was a fatally discourteous religion that disrupted the Pax Romana wherever it thrived.[2]

Tertullian understood why Christianity fell afoul of the empire. Christians refused to pay tribute to the gods, undermined the theological assumptions that upheld Rome's greatness, insulted the emperor, and appeared inhospitable to the empire and society. This made Christians an easy target for accusations of causing divine wrath, which would supposedly manifest in natural disasters or other calamities.

Criminals, both Christians and non-Christians, who undermined the peace of Rome often met their end in arenas and coliseums. These spaces, central to any good-sized Roman city, hosted public entertainments such as sporting events, mock battles, and executions.[3] These events served a mix of civic, penal, and religious purposes. In the Roman mind, the peace of the empire was a sign of divine favor, and disruptions invited divine punishment. Civic leaders not only maintained the social and economic life of the city but also frequently offered sacrifices for public benefit. Similarly, when criminals or enemies of Rome were publicly killed by trained fighters or exotic wild beasts, the events fulfilled both sacred and civic purposes. These spectacles reinforced Rome's supremacy and honored the gods through bloodshed.

In *De Spectaculis* (literally, "Of the Shows"), Tertullian argues that Christians should avoid public entertainments such as the circus,

---

2. MacCulloch, *Groundwork of Christian History*, 73.
3. B. Green, *Christianity in Ancient Rome*, 123.

amphitheater, theater, and arena. Although these events showcased aspects of God's creation—human strength, the beauty of animals, and musical voices—their perversion by the empire rendered them destructive to the spirit. Tertullian's argument against the shows is twofold: they are idolatrous festivals dedicated to pagan gods, and they are blood-soaked affairs unbecoming of Christian morality. Participation in the shows, he contends, is morally defiling and socially destructive.

Tertullian explicitly distinguishes between being in the world and participating in its pursuits:

> It is not by merely being in the world, however, that we lapse from God, but by touching and tainting ourselves with the world's sins. I shall break with my Maker, that is, by going to the Capitol or the temple of Serapis to sacrifice or adore, as I shall also do by going as a spectator to the circus and the theatre. The places in themselves do not contaminate, but what is done in them; from this even the places themselves, we maintain, become defiled. The polluted things pollute us.[4]

Tertullian's critique centers on the moral and spiritual pollution caused by the games and other public entertainments. Beyond morality, he also identifies psychological and social contamination. He writes:

> For as there is a lust of money, or rank, or eating, or impure enjoyment, or glory, so there is also a lust of pleasure. But the show is just a sort of pleasure. I think, then, that under the general designation of lusts, pleasures are included; in like manner, under the general idea of pleasures, you have as a specific class the "shows."[5]

The "lust" incited by the spectacles affects the will, redirecting desire away from the virtues encouraged by the Spirit and toward things that are "atrocious and vile."[6] He equates this with a "disfiguration of the human countenance, which is nothing less than the disfiguration of God's own image."[7] While individuals are morally and spiritually defiled, the broader community is also harmed by such pursuits.

The events depicted in the shows run contrary to public morality and undermine the foundations of a just society. Tertullian remarks, "The very

---

4. Tertullian, *De Spectaculis*, §7.
5. Tertullian, *De Spectaculis*, §14.
6. Tertullian, *De Spectaculis*, §12.
7. Tertullian, *De Spectaculis*, §18.

man who comes to the show, because he thinks murderers ought to suffer for their crime, drives the unwilling gladiator to the murderous deed with rods and scourges."[8] He concludes his argument by emphasizing that Christians should avoid these spectacles above all because they depict the very modes of execution used by the empire to crucify and torture Jesus Christ.[9]

In any culture, the church must ask, "How far can we go before being *in* the world becomes being *of* the world?" Tertullian's critique reflects the tension early Christians faced in navigating their fidelity to Christ while living in a society where even popular entertainments had religious dimensions.[10] For Tertullian, Christian involvement in such events was morally unacceptable, spiritually damaging, and socially corrosive. While participation tacitly condoned pagan civic-religious practices, the deeper issue was the impact of such events on the Christian's inner state.

One might argue that present-day sports fandom is radically different from Tertullian's context, as modern sporting events no longer serve an expressly religious function. However, idolatry was not Tertullian's only concern. Then, as now, sports and other entertainments often valorize violence and exalt competitiveness. For a faith that favors the meek and encourages passive resistance, these values seem contradictory to the gospel. Moreover, the bloodlust Tertullian observed persists in subtler forms today. Consider, for example, the death threats received by Howard Webb, the referee of the 2010 World Cup final, following controversial calls. Such incidents reveal a compelling continuity between Tertullian's experiences in third-century Carthage and ours in the twenty-first century.

SPORT AS MISSION

Tertullian represents one strand within Christianity that questions the propriety of Christians being involved in sport. Similar concerns have been echoed episodically throughout the church's history by traditions that view the relationship between Christianity and "secular" pursuits with suspicion. For example, medieval preachers often denounced the games accompanying festive gatherings as occasions for drunkenness, riot, and bloodshed.

---

8. Tertullian, *De Spectaculis*, §21.
9. Tertullian, *De Spectaculis*, §30.
10. B. Green, *Christianity in Ancient Rome*, 127.

Theology, Cultural Analysis, and Sport

Puritans worried about how sport and recreation could lure people away from godly activities into idleness and undisciplined living.[11]

Such anti-sport pundits expressed their views from a conservative theological worldview, seeking to separate faith and culture to preserve the purity of devotion to Christ. Involvement in sports, they argued, could taint faith and distract from the gospel. Yet, by the late nineteenth and early twentieth centuries, an opposite view emerged among equally conservative Christians who saw sports as a means to promote spiritual and moral discipline and proclaim the gospel. Rather than impeding the godly life, sports became central to Christian discipleship.

The rise of this theological shift is closely tied to the advent of "muscular Christianity" in the late nineteenth century. Popularized by authors like Charles Kingsley and Thomas Hughes, muscular Christianity emphasized traits such as physical fitness, valor, toughness, and self-reliance as essential to masculine identity. These ideals aligned with a broader cultural movement that lauded an adventurous spirit and downplayed sentimentality.

Though the provenance of the term "muscular Christianity" is debated, an early reference appeared in 1857 in a negative review of Charles Kingsley's novel *Two Years Ago* in the *Saturday Review*.[12] Kingsley's works, including the swashbuckling *Westward Ho!*, connected faith with physical prowess. *Westward Ho!* follows Amyas Leigh, a young man from North Devon who embarks on adventures on the high seas, battling pirates and Spaniards. The novel contrasts Englishness, Anglicanism, and hyper-masculinity with the perceived effeminacy of Spanish Catholics, whose Marian devotion is portrayed as weakening society. Such narratives contributed to the Victorian era's celebration of physical fitness and shaped an ideal of masculinity centered on self-reliance and endurance.

Alongside the rise of Kingsley's vision of masculinity, the Young Men's Christian Association (YMCA) was formed in 1844 as a Christian charity that aimed to provide healthy, productive, and spiritually uplifting opportunities for male youth in industrialized cities. Though initially YMCA's offerings centered around Bible study, eventually they took on a more sporty form. The first YMCA gymnasium was opened in London in 1888 to encourage youth to engage in physical fitness as a way of encouraging spiritual health by "both praying and playing."[13]

---

11. Chandler and Magdalinski, *God on Their Side*, 4.
12. Sanders, review of *Two Years Ago*.
13. Garnham, "Both Praying and Playing."

Section 2: Locations of Meaning Making

In his recent study, Clifford Putney highlights how, in America, the late Victorian emphasis on masculinity and religion responded to the perceived feminization of culture and excessive emotionalism in early nineteenth-century religion.[14] While this cultural shift spurred the rise of numerous fraternal organizations (e.g., the Odd Fellows, Freemasons), within the church, it led to a reimagining of masculine spirituality and even the masculinity of Jesus himself.

In many Christian books of the era, men were encouraged to follow Jesus' example of hard work, physical fitness, and self-reliance. In *The Masculine in Religion* (1906), Baptist minister Carl Delos Case likened the church to "a factory that turns out products for modern civilization . . . a laboratory examining soul life . . . an arsenal of armor for warfare . . . a foundry forging defensive armor . . . and a fort from which soldiers sally forth to victory."[15] Similarly, texts like Jason Pierce's *Masculine Power of Christ* (1912) and Harry Emerson Fosdick's *Manhood of the Master* (1913) argued that Christians should embrace a vigorous and muscular faith rather than being bogged down in dogma or creed.

Billy Sunday (1862–1935), the famed "baseball evangelist" (a former player for the Chicago White Sox), exemplified this vision. Sunday's charisma and physicality made him a prominent figure in American Evangelicalism. In a 1916 interview with the *Trenton Evening Times*, Sunday declared: "Jesus Christ intended his church to be militant as well as persuasive. It must fight as well as pray. . . . Strong men resist; weaklings compromise. Lord, save us from off-handed, flabby-cheeked, brittle-boned, weak-kneed, thin-skinned, pliable, plastic, spineless, effeminate, sissified, three-carat Christianity."[16] For Sunday, true manhood was epitomized in following Jesus Christ.

By the early twentieth century, the explicit label of muscular Christianity had waned, but its ideals were absorbed into broader cultural norms. The emphasis on physical fitness and moral integrity continued, becoming embedded in institutions promoting sports, outdoor activities, and character education.

The legacy of muscular Christianity created an environment in which Christianity and sports were seen as compatible and mutually beneficial.

---

14. Putney, *Muscular Christianity*, 24.

15. Case, *Masculine in Religion*, 84.

16. Billy Sunday, "The Fighting Saint," *Trenton [New Jersey] Evening Times*, Jan. 6, 1916; as quoted in DeBerg, *Ungodly Women*, 89.

In 1954, Elizabeth Nottingham coined the phrase "basketballization of the churches" to describe the proliferation of church-based gymnasiums in the United States.[17] Today, many family-friendly churches either include gymnasiums or meet in multipurpose spaces that function as both sanctuaries and gyms, dubbed "sanctanasiums."

In the 1970s, American evangelist Billy Graham remarked: "The Bible says leisure and lying around are morally dangerous for us. Sports keep us busy; athletes, you notice, don't take drugs. There are probably more really committed Christians in sports, both collegiate and professional, than in any other occupation in America."[18] Graham (following the tone set by the YMCA a century before) saw sport as a positive diversion that keeps kids out of trouble. More than just something to occupy the hands and minds or as a way of encouraging discipline, participation, and community, sports from the 1970s became a key means of engaging in evangelism for the local church. As sports grew in cultural popularity, the attitude to sports in American churches changed dramatically. What was once a practice taken up by the lazy became a way of encouraging discipline and participation and, by the 1970s, was a key mode of communicating the gospel in a culturally relevant fashion.

Today, "sports as evangelism" continues within the life of the church. Several international organizations specifically minister to those involved in professional sports: Baseball Chapel provides pregame chapel services to American baseball players; the Motor Racing Outreach ministers to professional NASCAR drivers; and in the UK many professional football clubs hire chaplains to nurture the spiritual lives of their players. Indeed, it's not only among professionals that religion has made a significant inroad; collegiate and semiprofessional sporting clubs boast several religious networks that seek to foster the spiritual lives of athletes (e.g., Fellowship of Christian Athletes; Athletes in Action). Even the spiritual needs of anglers (Fellowship of Christian Anglers), motorcyclists (Christian Motorcyclists Association), and jockeys (Race Track Chaplaincy of America) are catered to. In a fascinating exploration of this trend, one scholar quips that "never has so much evangelical ammunition been fired by so many at so few."[19]

---

17. Nottingham, *Religion and Society*, 78.
18. B. Graham, "Sports Good for the Soul?," 51.
19. Hoffman, "Toward Narrowing the Gulf," 307.

Section 2: Locations of Meaning Making

SPORTS AS A RELIGION

Another way of understanding sports is not as a distinct or separate cultural form from religion but as something historically and inherently religious or religion-like in itself. Beyond Tertullian's connection between Greco-Roman mythology and athletic competitions, there is a compelling argument that sports originated as part of religious rituals intended to influence the gods, promote fertility, and secure an abundant harvest. In ancient Central America, for instance, Mayans played a basketball-like game overseen by priests in fields attached to temples. Native Americans played an early form of lacrosse to divine the future. Sumo wrestling tournaments in Japan incorporated Shinto purification rites (e.g., throwing salt) and reflected Shinto's hierarchical values. This association between sports and rites of worship persisted into the Christian Middle Ages, where religious festivals often included games and competitions that framed participants within a cosmic narrative of good versus evil and the kingdom of God.[20]

At the beginning of this chapter, I reflected on my experience attending a professional American football game. The atmosphere—the loss of individual inhibitions, the surrender to group dynamics, and the role of sports in shaping value and identity—bears a striking resemblance to what sociologist Émile Durkheim described in Aboriginal Australian gatherings called corroborees. Durkheim writes:

> The very fact of the concentration [of individuals] acts as an exceptionally powerful stimulant. When they are once come together, a sort of electricity is formed by the collecting which quickly transports them to an extraordinary degree of exaltation. Every sentiment expressed finds a place without resistance in all the minds, which are very open to outside impressions; each re-echoes the others, and is re-echoed by the others. The initial impulse thus proceeds, growing as it goes, as an avalanche grows in its advance. And as such passions so free from all control could not fail to burst out, on every side one sees nothing but violent gestures, cries, veritable howls, and deafening noises of every sort, which intensify still more the state of mind which they manifest. And since a collective sentiment cannot express itself collectively except on the condition of observing a certain order permitting co-operation and movements in unison, these gestures and cries

---

20. Hoffman, *Sport and Religion*, 144.

naturally tend to become rhythmic and regular; hence come songs and dances.[21]

According to his functionalist definition of religion, Durkheim regarded such gatherings as explicitly religious events that convey a sense of the sacred, communicate moral principles, and strengthen society. While Durkheim's methodology for studying religion is subject to critique, his functionalist theory remains widely influential in the comparative study of religion across cultures.[22] Using this approach, we can identify phenomena as religious or religion-like even if they do not involve belief in a deity or explicitly identify as religious.

Applying Durkheimian functionalism to sports reveals numerous compelling religious traits. For example, in both sports and religion, masses regularly gather at designated sites (stadiums or houses of worship) to focus their attention on the activities of a small group of representatives (players or priests). These representatives perform actions guided by key principles and patterns (rule books or liturgies) handed down by tradition and interpreted by a select elite (officials or clergy). Participants in both realms often wear distinctive clothing (jerseys or vestments), and adherents own or bring objects that reinforce their devotion (sports memorabilia or religious symbols like crosses or prayer beads). Additionally, both sports and religion have places set apart for veneration (trophy rooms or shrines) where visitors honor exemplary figures (MVPs or saints) and gaze upon their associated artifacts (balls or jerseys or relics).

Both sports and religion emphasize personal testimony, where individuals recount transformative or significant experiences (sports stories or faith testimonies). Moreover, both spheres have zealots and fanatics who prioritize their devotion above all else, and both are historically dominated by men.

From a functionalist perspective, sports fulfill many of the roles traditionally associated with religion. They draw people into cohesive communities; offer transcendent experiences of well-being, mystery, awe, and unity; and provide a sense of story, myth, and metaphor. For example, a marathoner training tirelessly through adverse weather, illness, or personal sacrifice embodies the same dedication, sacrifice, and commitment as a devout daily churchgoer who prioritizes their spiritual practices over worldly

---

21. Durkheim, *Elementary Forms*, 246–47.
22. Pals, *Seven Theories of Religion*, 281.

goals. Both pursuits reveal a devotion to a higher ideal, whether framed in terms of personal excellence or divine worship.[23]

CONCLUSION: SPORTS AND THEOLOGICAL REFLECTION

What are we to say about all of this if we turn our attention to the methodology advanced at the start of this book? Is sporting an expression of Ultimate Concern? Is it a means by which God reveals Godself to us? Is sport its own kind of religion, quite different from the religious milieu of the Bible or the church? Is participation in sports problematic for Christians (surfacing Tertullian's concerns, noted at the start of this chapter)? Are the values of sports (masculinity, muscularity, competitiveness) the sorts of virtues we want to cultivate as part of the Christian life? Should sports be used as a way of evangelizing, either by making the church more sports friendly or by pursuing chaplaincy opportunities that meet the needs of particular groups of athletes? What do we make of this very complicated mixing of theology and everyday life?

By way of conclusion, I want to offer three thoughts on embodiment, community, and play, which I hope offer a middle ground between an all-out ban on Christian sporting (on the one hand) and the seeming replacement of religious faith and practice by sports, which seems plausible in the stadium on any given Sunday.

Embodiment

Intrinsic to Tertullian's critique of sports is a concern with maintaining the purity of the soul. Since I grew up in a church that associated spiritual purity with sexual abstinence (twentieth-century Pentecostals were very much modern-day descendants of second-century Montanists), his logic sounds remarkably familiar to me. And yet, his anthropology—that is, his theological understanding of what it means to be human—rests heavily on the foundation of Hellenistic duality, which separates the body and the soul. The soul must remain pure and untouched by the passions, desires, and activities of the body. This view, however, begins from a position that regards embodiment as suspect, dangerous, and inherently (or dispositionally) sinful. Such a view, while remarkably persistent in the history of the

---

23. Prebish, *Religion and Sport*, 63.

church, is certainly foreign to the theological imagination of much of the Scriptures, which begin by framing material, human, creaturely existence as inherently "good." The goodness of the body (of exercise, labor, play, sex, etc.) is something that twentieth- and twenty-first-century theologians have endeavored to recover and which, though not without problems, is a positive contribution made by sporting approaches to faith.

Community

Sporting absolutely can build community. The bonds shared among the team, by fans, and passed on from generations are truly remarkable. And also, sports can become a divisive force that undermines the broader call of God for the creation of a united and beloved community. I'm reminded of a story from when I lived in Aberdeen, Scotland. A child of about nine or ten was playing in the park and wearing an England football jersey (which, to be fair, is a bit of a foolish thing for a parent to dress their child in if you're living in the northeast of Scotland). The child was approached by a young man, probably in his early twenties, and told that he needed to take off that disgraceful shirt. When the child refused, a fight ensued, which led to the young man's arrest and the child being rushed to the hospital with minor injuries. While the community created by sports is laudable, when this community divides rather than unites, it no longer serves a positive end.

Play

Intrinsic to the Puritan critique of sports is a concern for productivity and work over the value of rest. Yet, while sporting is a recreational activity, it can still become so central in one's life that it ceases to be restorative, restful, and playful and becomes just another job or activity that drives us to perform and produce. Perhaps situating sport within the context of a notion of Sabbath or within the broader framework of "play" may help us, on both sides of the argument, to see sporting as a way in which we seek joy and rest in the midst of our daily lives and perhaps to see something of the promise of the eschatological Sabbath to which we are oriented.

The interplay between sports and theological reflection invites us to consider deeply the values we champion as part of our faith and how these manifest in the wider cultural practices we engage in, particularly sports. As we reflect on embodiment, community, and play, we find that sports offer not only a field for physical expression but also a platform for spiritual and communal growth. They challenge us to reimagine the sacredness of the body, the power of community to both unite and divide, and the vital role of play in our spiritual lives. In navigating the complexities of sports within a Christian framework, we are called to a balanced approach that recognizes the potential for sports to embody and teach the virtues of the gospel, while also being mindful of the ways in which they can stray from or conflict with our core beliefs. Ultimately, engaging with sports as part of our theological journey can lead us to a richer understanding of our faith, a deeper appreciation of our embodiment, and a more profound sense of community and play in our lives, all of which draw us closer to the eschatological promise of rest and unity in God's eternal kingdom.

5

Formed Theology
Transformation Through Making

WHEN MY WIFE, JULIA, and I were dating and in our first years of college, we discovered a mutual love for ceramics (and each other!). The campus studio where we spent countless hours was its own world, tucked at the edge of campus, down a winding staircase leading to a brutalist concrete building. Inside, the hum of spinning wheels, the smell of wet clay, and the promise of transformation filled the air. Shelves crowded with greenware, glaze bottles, and dog-eared art books created a space alive with creative energy. Even now, the smell of an autumn burn pile reminds me of those raku firings by the rolling metal door of the kiln room, where we plunged red-hot pots into sawdust and leaves, watching the flames leap and smoke billow.

At the time, ceramics was a journey of discovery and expression—a medium through which I, despite my poor hand-eye coordination, somehow managed to create beauty. We made pots, jars, and platters, many of which were packed away after graduation. Yet we never lost the sense that working with clay was grounding, embodying a connection to something both earthy and transcendent. Life moved on, and so did we, leaving our creations to gather dust in the attic, tucked away with our clay tools and aprons.

Years later, in the midst of the COVID-19 pandemic, we found our way back to pottery almost on a whim. Julia was the first to rekindle her connection with the craft, taking occasional classes at a local ceramics studio. Before long, I joined her at the wheel. I resumed throwing just as I stepped into the demanding role of dean and president at my seminary. As the weight of institutional leadership pressed down on me, we dusted off old memories, bought a wheel, and carved out a workspace in a damp, underutilized basement office on the seminary campus. The room, prone to flooding and cluttered with remnants of a preschool that was abandoned during the pandemic, was far from ideal. And yet, it became a refuge—a place to rediscover the rhythms of making and the joy of transformation.

Working with clay again awakened something deep within me—not just as a potter but as a theologian and a priest. Reclaiming clay from scraps, wedging it into readiness, and centering it on the wheel became a living parable of creation and redemption. In the Genesis accounts of creation, we encounter two perspectives on divine creativity: the commanding fiat that calls creation into existence (Gen 1) and the intimate, tactile act of forming humanity from dust (Gen 2–3). Working with clay felt like rediscovering that latter image, where creation is not abstract but embodied, relational, and teeming with potential. The plasticity of clay, with its nearly unlimited capacity for renewal, reminded me that even in my own brokenness and limitations, God's patient and persistent care can bring purpose out of failure.

MAKING AS EMBODIED THEOLOGY

Making with clay is inherently an embodied activity. It resists abstraction and demands presence—a full attentiveness of mind and body, an openness to the clay's resistance and its possibilities. You can't learn to wedge clay or center it on a wheel from a textbook; you must sense its readiness in the rhythm of your movements and feel the clay's wobble under your hands. Even when you've learned basic ceramic techniques, clay retains its fragility. Like humanity awaiting its ultimate redemption, pottery is prone to collapse, to crack, or to be reshaped by the forces it endures. The very nature of the craft demands resilience and forgiveness—not just for the clay but for the potter. Mistakes are inevitable: walls collapse, glazes misfire, pieces crack in the kiln. And yet, clay's infinite recyclability is a reminder of grace. A collapsed pot can be reclaimed, a shattered vessel can be mended with *kintsugi*, its scars adorned with gold.

In our small studio, clay moves through its own life cycle: from slurry to slab, from wedging table to wheel, from drying shelf to kiln. Even the ugliest of cups can still hold water, and the humblest of creations bear beauty. Working with clay has taught me to let go of perfectionism, to embrace failure as part of the process, and to find joy in the ordinary. It has become, in a very real sense, a spiritual discipline—a practice that forms and reforms the maker even as the maker shapes the clay.

THE THEOLOGY OF EVERYDAY MAKING

There is a tendency to treat the arts as the preserve of the talented or to measure the worth of craft by arbitrary notions of perfection or beauty. While there is, of course, much to admire in the fine porcelain vase displayed in a museum, my interest lies elsewhere. I'm drawn to the beauty of the everyday: the jug left in the corner of a barn, the pitcher that cries for water to carry.[1] It's the kind of beauty that Soetsu Yanagi celebrates in *The Beauty of Everyday Things*—a beauty born of simplicity, utility, and the rhythm of life. For Yanagi, the finest crafts are not those made for admiration but those that find their fullness in use: the bowls that hold rice, the mugs that bear tea. These objects, crafted not for fame but for purpose, hold an unpretentious grace that reflects the hands of the anonymous maker and the life of the intended user.

This chapter explores theology and the arts through the lens of making. Art here is not an elite or isolated act but an ordinary, everyday practice that has served, for me and for countless others, as a means of divine self-disclosure. My focus is less on aesthetics and more on what can be learned in the everyday process of making itself. To this end, we'll begin by looking at the presence of handicraft in Scripture and the Christian imagination. From the myths of creation or Marian fabric craft, the Bible offers rich metaphors of making, grounding human creativity in everyday life. From there, we'll turn to recent theological writing, noting how much work in this area privileges either a hermeneutic approach—treating art as something to be interpreted—or an aesthetic one, valuing art for its beauty or transcendence. While these approaches have their merits, they often overlook what I call a practice-based theology of making: one that finds meaning not in the finished product but in the act of creation itself.

Finally, I'll share some of my own experiences of developing a practice-based spirituality of making, what I have come to call *fabricandi divina*, or "divine making." This is not about achieving perfection or producing objects of admiration. It's about engaging with the material world in ways that are grounded, transformative, and deeply human. As we explore these themes, I invite you to think about making as something far more democratic than

1. Piercy, "To Be of Use."

it's often imagined—a way for all to participate in the rhythms of creation. Whether it's pottery, knitting, cooking, or gardening, the act of making teaches us something about God, ourselves, and the world. It's not just about what we create but how we are formed in the process.

THE CHRISTIAN IMAGINATION AND MAKING

The Genesis of Making

Every culture wonders why there is something rather than nothing. For ancient Israel, as for other peoples of the ancient Near East, the question of origins was not just about the mechanics of the universe but about its meaning. The two creation stories in Gen 1–3 reflect this theological concern, offering a view of a world that is shaped by a God who blesses creation and entrusts humanity with its care.

In the broader narrative of Gen 1–11, the focus moves from God's creative acts (Gen 1–3) to humanity's role in shaping the world (Gen 4–11). By Gen 4, the text presents a world in which humans must innovate and create to survive. Culture is portrayed not as a divine gift but as the result of human agency. Unlike creation myths such as the Sumerian Myth of the Pick Axe,[2] where tools and technologies are explicitly divine inventions imbued with sacred significance, Genesis situates these developments firmly in human hands. In the story immediately following the first episode of fratricide in Scripture, the so-called lineage of Cain, early archetypal figures like Jabal, Jubal, and Tubal-Cain are credited with foundational advances in material culture: livestock herding, music, and metallurgy (Gen 4:17–26).

Westermann observes that this inclusion early in the Genesis "desacralizes human cultural progress from the very beginning."[3] As such, music, agriculture, urban planning, or metallurgy are regarded as achievements that emerge from human creativity and effort and not separate divine acts of creation. This seems to harken back to God's original blessing to "be fruitful and multiply" (Gen 1:28), which places responsibility for the cultivation of the world squarely on human shoulders. This theological move elevates the dignity of human making and underscores the trust God places in humanity as stewards of creation.

---

2. Jeremy Black et al., *Literature of Ancient Sumer*.
3. Westermann, *Genesis 1–11*, 67.

The tension between creativity and moral failure runs through Gen 1–11, particularly in the story of Cain's lineage. The genealogy of Jabal, Jubal, and Tubal-Cain celebrates human ingenuity, yet it concludes with the song of Lamech, which seems to almost boastfully recount vengeance and violence. This duality illustrates the ambivalence of human making, which can mirror the creativity of the imago Dei but also be marred by sin and violence. Human making, then, is not inherently good or bad but carries the ethical responsibility to align with God's purposes.

This perspective aligns with the broader themes of Gen 1–11, where freedom and accountability define humanity's role in creation. Like God, who creates ex nihilo in Gen 1 and shapes humanity from dust in Gen 2, humans are makers. Yet human making is bound by limitations, prone to both brilliance and failure. Westermann emphasizes that "it is the person who is blessed; the person who does the work." Genesis 4 invites us to see making as an essential part of human life—an everyday act that reflects both the promise of divine blessing and the risk of human brokenness.

Exodus: The Spirit and Creativity

In high school and college, I was deeply shaped by the Pentecostal tradition, where the Spirit's work was understood as a dynamic and transformative force in the life of believers. Central to this theology was the "baptism in the Holy Spirit," a second blessing that followed water baptism. This experience was believed to be marked by the initial evidence of speaking in tongues, signifying a Spirit-filled life characterized by holiness and spiritual gifts. In this context, the Spirit's presence was most often associated with charismatic phenomena, emphasizing God's direct and immediate intervention in the lives of individuals.

Over the decades, my understanding of the Spirit's work has broadened and deepened. Now, as a priest in the Episcopal Church, I encounter the Spirit's presence in ways that are no less transformative but often more subtly woven into the fabric of communal worship, sacramental life, and creation itself. The prayer at confirmation, spoken by the bishop of the confirmand, encapsulates this expansive vision of the Spirit's role: "Strengthen, O Lord, your servant N. with your Holy Spirit; empower him for your service; and sustain him all the days of his life. Amen."[4]

---

4. Episcopal Church, *Book of Common Prayer*, 418.

Section 2: Locations of Meaning Making

This prayer evokes the Spirit's empowering and sustaining presence in the life of the church, echoing the Pentecostal emphasis on empowerment but embedding it within the broader rhythms of sacramental and liturgical life. Yet, it is significant to note, especially in the context of this chapter, that the first person described in Scripture as being "filled with the Spirit" was neither a prophet nor a confirmand but an artisan: Bezalel. His Spirit-filled work was not glossolalia or miracles but craftsmanship—creating the sacred objects for the tabernacle. This insight invites a broader understanding of the Spirit's activity, one that encompasses not only spiritual gifts but also the artistry and creativity that reflect God's own creative nature.

> See, I have called by name Bezalel the son of Uri, son of Hur, of the tribe of Judah, and I have filled him with the Spirit of God, with ability and intelligence, with knowledge and all craftsmanship, to devise artistic designs, to work in gold, silver, and bronze, in cutting stones for setting, and in carving wood, to work in every craft. (Exod 31:2–5)

In this passage, the Spirit's filling is directly tied to material culture. Bezalel is charged, alongside Oholiab, with crafting the tabernacle, the ark of the covenant, and the sacred furnishings for Israel's worship. The tasks assigned to these artisans emphasize the sacred purpose of their craftsmanship. They are to work with gold, silver, bronze, wood, and fabric to create intricate designs, from the tent of meeting to the priestly garments. This narrative elevates human making, showing that ordinary skills can be consecrated to serve divine purposes.

John Goldingay suggests that Bezalel and Oholiab's talents were not invented by the Spirit but commissioned and elevated:

> Bezalel will not have been someone who was hopeless at metalwork to whom God now gave this gift; he is someone with such gifts whom God now commissions to do the work that is needed.[5]

His reflection points to the partnership between divine initiative and human skill. Bezalel and Oholiab's skills were already present, rooted in everyday material culture, but the Spirit's presence elevated their work to something more. The passage from Exod 31 also emphasizes the communal aspect of creativity. While Bezalel and Oholiab are named, God gives "all able" people the ability to contribute. This reflects the collaborative nature of sacred craftsmanship: the tabernacle was not built by a single genius but

---

5. Goldingay, *Exodus and Leviticus*, 111.

by a community working together, inspired by the Spirit. This communal effort underscores that making, even when infused with divine purpose, is not about individual acclaim but about collective service.

MARY: WEAVER OF THE DIVINE

In modern-day Nazareth, a steep, narrow street connects two sacred landmarks. At the bottom sits the sprawling Basilica of the Annunciation, a massive complex commemorating the moment when Mary received Gabriel's message that she would bear the Son of God. Inside and out, the church's walls are adorned with mosaics of the Virgin Mary reflecting nearly every nation's imagination—from the vibrant red-and-black Cameroonian to the golden Thai Virgin—all celebrating how Mary's story has taken root in the hearts of believers across the globe.

At the top of the street is Christ Church (Anglican), a smaller but no less significant church, serving the mostly Arab-Palestinian Christian community of Nazareth. Its clean, cream-colored stones and familiar architecture make it reminiscent of Anglican parish churches worldwide. Behind its altar is a reredos with an Arabic inscription quoting Jesus' reading from Isa 61, recounted in Luke 4:14–30—an event that nearly saw him thrown off a cliff in his own hometown:

> The Spirit of the Lord is upon me,
> because he has anointed me
> to bring good news to the poor.
> He has sent me to proclaim release to the captives
> and recovery of sight to the blind,
> to let the oppressed go free,
> to proclaim the year of the Lord's favor. (Luke 4:18–19)

Between these two landmarks is situated an unassuming convent, the home of the Sisters of Nazareth. I visited this convent with a friend who had arranged for us to view a seldom-visited archaeological site beneath it. What we found buried under the convent was extraordinary: a well-preserved first-century home. This dwelling, complete with a stone-cut manger that might have held food for animals—or perhaps a small child—was surrounded by spaces that could have been a carpenter's or mason's workshop. Some believe this was Jesus' childhood home. While it is impossible to confirm such claims, the site offers a vivid window into domestic life in first-century Nazareth.

Section 2: Locations of Meaning Making

Among the artifacts recovered from the site, displayed in a modest museum above the ruins, was a simple yet fascinating object: a small stone spindle whorl. About three inches in diameter at its widest, it resembled a toy top with a pointed base and a roughly carved eyelet at the top. This tool was used for spinning wool into yarn. My wife, both a potter and a fabric artist, recognized it immediately—she had learned to spin yarn with a nearly identical spindle made of wood before acquiring her spinning wheel. Remarkably, this ancient tool bears a striking resemblance to similar spindles still in use around the world today.

Whether this spindle belonged to Mary or not, its inclusion in the museum's collection evokes the long-standing tradition that associates Mary with fabric craft. While the Gospels provide few details about Jesus' early domestic life, the early church filled in these gaps with stories and legends, drawing on its theological imagination to reflect on the hidden years of Mary and Jesus. One significant source for these traditions was the Protevangelium of James, an apocryphal text from the second century.

The Protevangelium of James did not make its way into the biblical canon, likely due to its late authorship (estimated mid-second century) and lack of apostolic influence. Despite this, it shaped Christian art, devotion, and theology, particularly during the medieval era. Its influence can be seen in countless ways, from art to poetry, as it offers a vivid and imaginative expansion on the life of Mary, enriching traditions that later informed her veneration.

For example, the text introduces us to the traditional names of Mary's parents, Joachim and Anne, who became central figures in the Christian tradition. Their portrayal as elderly, devout, and miraculously blessed with a child after years of barrenness mirrors biblical accounts of similarly miraculous births, such as Sarah with Isaac and Hannah with Samuel. This parallel underscores Mary's unique and providential role in salvation history, later informing the doctrine of her immaculate conception.

The Protevangelium expands on Mary's early life, describing her dedication to the temple as a child, where she lived until her betrothal to Joseph. During this time, Mary is depicted as engaging in sacred work, including spinning and weaving the veil for the temple—a symbolic act that underscores her connection to the divine and her pivotal role in the unfolding plan of salvation (Prot. Jas. 10). This act of weaving can be interpreted as a metaphor for her future role in "weaving" the flesh of Christ in her womb, highlighting her sanctity and active participation in God's work.

This depiction of Mary as a young girl engaged in fabric craft has inspired countless artistic renderings, including the Master of Erfurt's *The Virgin Weaving* (1400s), Van Eyck's *Annunciation* (1430s), and Leonardo da Vinci's *Madonna of the Yarnwinder* (1501), as well as a wide range of unattributed pieces such as *The Virgin Embroidering with Saints Anne and Joachim* (Bolivian, 1600s) and *Virgin Mary Spinning* (Spanish, ca. 1700). These images often portray Mary accompanied by the tools of fabric craft or standing at the steps of the temple during her childhood—motifs symbolizing her unique holiness, her dedication to God, and her foreshadowed role as the Theotokos (God-bearer).

Mary's association with weaving offers rich theological insights. The act of weaving, like spinning clay or crafting wood, is deeply material and embodied. It reflects the integration of the divine and the human, the eternal and the temporal. In Mary's case, this is not only metaphorical but literal: in her womb, God took on human flesh. The spindle whorl found in the Sisters of Nazareth convent reminds us that Mary's life, though extraordinary, was also deeply ordinary. She cooked meals, spun yarn, and engaged in the everyday work of first-century domestic life. Yet, through her willingness to say yes to God's call, her ordinary life became the means of extraordinary grace.

What does the story of Mary as a weaver teach us about the theology of making? First, it underscores the sacredness of the ordinary. The tools and tasks of domestic life—spindles, looms, clay, and wood—become instruments of divine purpose when placed in the hands of the faithful. Second, it highlights the interplay of divine and human agency. Mary's weaving, like Bezalel's craftsmanship, is both a human effort and a participation in God's redemptive work. Finally, Mary's story invites us to view making not merely as a functional act but as a spiritual practice. Whether we are spinning wool, shaping clay, or engaging in any creative endeavor, the act of making may well draw us into deeper communion with God, reminding us that the extraordinary often begins in the ordinary.

ARTS IN THEOLOGY AND THEOLOGY IN THE ARTS

The relationship between theology and the arts has long been a fruitful one, offering insights into the divine-human relationship, the nature of creation, and the mystery of existence. This rich dialogue unfolds across a spectrum

Section 2: Locations of Meaning Making

of approaches, each offering insight into the interplay between human creativity and theology. Such approaches include:

- Theological aesthetics: Scholars like Hans Urs von Balthasar explore how beauty reveals divine truth, emphasizing the role of aesthetics in theology.[6]
- Art as theology: Jeremy Begbie highlights how music, painting, and other forms open new avenues for understanding God, using art as a source for theological reflection.[7]
- Cultural and religious content: Thinkers such as David Morgan examine the religious content within art, analyzing its cultural and theological significance.[8]
- Practical theology: This approach investigates how art not only reflects but also shapes communal worship, spiritual practices, and ethical considerations in religious contexts. Scholars like Robin M. Jensen explore how art functions in worship and liturgy, emphasizing its role in shaping theological understanding through visual and material culture. William Dyrness investigates how the arts contribute to spiritual practices and communal identity, particularly within liturgical traditions. Meanwhile, thinkers such as Stephen B. Bevans and Frank Burch Brown highlight the ethical and theological implications of art in worship, including its potential commodification and misuse.[9]
- Dynamic interplay: Scholars like S. Brent Plate study the connections between art, culture, and spirituality, enriching our understanding of how art functions as a site of meaning making and divine encounter.[10]

---

6. Balthasar, *Seeing the Form*. This volume introduces Balthasar's comprehensive vision of beauty as central to divine revelation and theological inquiry.

7. Begbie, *Voicing Creation's Praise* and *Resounding Truth*. These works explore how music and other arts facilitate theological reflection and deepen our understanding of God.

8. Morgan, *Visual Piety* and *Forge of Vision*. Morgan analyzes the cultural and theological dimensions of visual art and its role in shaping religious thought and practice.

9. Jensen, *Substance of Things Seen*; Dyrness, *Poetic Theology*; Dyrness, *Visual Faith*; Brown, *Good Taste, Bad Taste*; Bevans and Schroeder, *Prophetic Dialogue*.

10. Plate, *Walter Benjamin* and *Religion, Art, Visual Culture*. These works explore how art mediates sacred experiences, highlighting the cultural and spiritual dimensions of artistic practices and their impact on the practice of religion.

While these perspectives offer a rich tapestry of insights, apart from the work of Plate and Morgan, much of the scholarship focuses on the finished work of art—the painting, the sculpture, the composition—often privileging high art over the everyday process of making. This emphasis can overshadow the theological potential inherent in ordinary acts of creativity. While these approaches provide significant contributions, they risk neglecting the theological insights that come along with the act of creation itself or restrict their analysis to the work of more professional artists, overlooking more domestic forms of handicraft.

Perhaps one problem inherent to the study of theology and the arts is the peculiar distinction made between "art" and "craft," particularly in English. Art is often associated with individual genius and aesthetic transcendence, while craft is linked to utility, community, and domesticity. This dichotomy marginalizes forms of making that do not conform to elite or classist definitions of artistry. Feminist scholars like Rozsika Parker have critiqued this divide, highlighting how domestic handicrafts such as embroidery have been historically devalued despite their cultural and creative significance. Parker argues that reclaiming these crafts can challenge patriarchal and classist hierarchies, offering alternative ways to engage with beauty, community, and spirituality.[11]

Ceramics, like Parker's understanding of fabric craft, challenges the bifurcation between art and craft. A ceramic vessel—whether a museum-worthy porcelain vase or a crude jug discovered in the back of a barn—reflects both utility and beauty. The works of the enslaved African American artist David Drake, known historically as Dave the Potter, exemplify this intersection. His ceramic vessels, now prized in American art museums, were originally functional objects—pickling jars or storage jugs—but also bear poetic inscriptions that elevate them beyond utility to prized works of art. These pieces invite reflection on the ethical and spiritual dimensions of making, where the practical and the creative are inextricably linked. By bridging the divide between *praxis* (action) and *poiesis* (creation), ceramics democratizes the act of making, inviting both novices and masters into a shared practice that is accessible and deeply human.

While theological aesthetics often highlight the finished artwork, ceramics uniquely invites us to reflect on the act of making itself—a process that readily reflects theological principles such as incarnation, redemption, and community. Unlike many other art forms, ceramics sits at the

---

11. Parker, *Subversive Stitch*.

intersection of beauty and utility, offering insights into the sacredness of ordinary acts of creation.

Ceramics offers a uniquely fertile context for theological reflection and practice, embodying characteristics that make it particularly suited for exploring the spiritual dimensions of making. First, ceramics bridges the divide between "high" and "low" art, providing a space where beauty and function coexist. This integration challenges hierarchical notions of artistic value and affirms the sacredness of ordinary acts of making that permeate daily life. Moreover, ceramics is profoundly democratic; while mastery requires a lifetime of practice, even a novice can shape a simple bowl or cup. This accessibility invites everyone, regardless of skill level, to move from being a passive consumer to an active participant in creation.

The physicality of ceramics further deepens its theological resonance. From wedging clay to centering it on the wheel, the process demands physical engagement, linking the maker to the material world in ways that resonate with the Christian emphasis on incarnation and embodied spirituality. This practice also connects us to the broader arc of human history. As one of the oldest art forms, ceramics grounds theological reflection in the tangible realities of ancient life, offering insights into the cultural and domestic contexts of biblical narratives.

Practices such as *wabi-sabi* and *kintsugi*, rooted in Japanese aesthetics and Zen philosophy, offer rich themes of imperfection, restoration, and simplicity. While these concepts emerge from a distinct spiritual and cultural tradition, they resonate deeply with Christian notions of sin, grace, and redemption. Engaging these practices invites an interfaith dialogue that expands our theological imagination while respecting their unique cultural origins. In this way, ceramics becomes a bridge—not only between art and craft but also between cultures, histories, and spiritualities—inviting theological exploration that is both grounded and expansive. It democratizes creativity, embodying themes of incarnation and grace through its tangible, accessible nature. By forming with clay, the maker enters a process that mirrors and illuminates spiritual and theological formation. The experience of risk, failure, renewal, and transformation in ceramics parallels the dynamics of grace, repentance, and redemption. In its interplay with cross-cultural practices and its resonance with the rhythms of everyday life, ceramics becomes a vessel—not just for function or beauty but for exploring the connections between creation, community, and the Creator.

CONCLUSION: AN EXAMPLE OF A PRACTICE-BASED THEOLOGY OF MAKING

In late 2024, Julia and I applied to the Episcopal Evangelism Society for a modest grant to expand our studio's capacity. Up to that point, we had been firing all our creations in what we affectionately called "the world's smallest kiln," a firebrick box measuring just eight inches by eight inches on the inside. The grant would allow us to purchase a production kiln, enabling the studio to welcome a wider community of makers. For us, this was more than a logistical upgrade; it was a step toward realizing a vision of sharing the joy of making and the spiritual lessons we've learned through it with our neighbors and my students.

Our first experiment in teaching spirituality through clay came with a group of eighteen people from St. Peter's Church. On a Wednesday night, we gathered for a simple meal before transitioning into the studio to make hand crosses. The process was guided by what I called *fabricandi divina*—holy making—a practice inspired by the meditative rhythms of *lectio divina* but reimagined for the tactile, creative act of shaping clay.

Fabricandi divina invites participants to encounter God in the ordinary act of making, reflecting the theological themes of formation, transformation, and divine grace. Through its stages—*formatio, conformatio, ornatum, contemplatio*, and *traditio*—participants are drawn into a rhythm of creation that mirrors their spiritual journey. The process echoes the theology explored in this chapter: that making is both a reflection of the imago Dei and a means of experiencing, in tangible forms, God's ongoing work of redemption.

As the evening began, I invited everyone to gather around a long table in the studio. We opened with a prayer, asking for God's presence in our work, and I explained how the process of *fabricandi divina* would unfold—a sacred rhythm of making that was grounded in the tactile, earthy act of shaping clay.

Formatio (Formation): Preparing the Clay

We began with the clay itself, inviting participants to hold it in their hands, exploring its texture, resistance, and malleability. I read aloud from Gen 2:7, the story of God forming humanity from the dust of the earth. "Take a moment," I said, "to feel the clay in your hands and reflect on how God is shaping you. What areas of your life feel dry or hardened? Where might you need to be softened or remolded?"

Some participants closed their eyes, their hands moving rhythmically as they worked the clay. Others stared at the lump, either challenged by a new task or lost in thought. This simple beginning set the tone for the evening: a reminder that we, too, are works in progress, continually shaped by the hands of our Creator.

Conformatio (Shaping): Cutting and Shaping the Cross

Next, we formed the crosses. Participants rolled out their clay and used a simple template to cut and shape it. As we worked, I shared the words of Isa 64:8: "We are the clay, and you are our potter; we are all the work of your hand." "This cross," I explained, "is a symbol of your spiritual journey. As you shape it, think about the burdens and blessings you carry. What does this moment in your life look like? What do you bring to this cross, and what does it say about who you are in Christ?" The room grew quiet, save for the soft scrape of tools on clay. Some participants worked quickly, while others hesitated, shaping their pieces slowly and with care. The results were as varied as the people in the room: some formed simple hand crosses, others etched intricate designs, while still others created crosses inspired by Celtic or Coptic traditions.

Ornatum (Adornment): Pressing and Decorating

Once the crosses were shaped, participants began to adorn them. I encouraged everyone to press designs or symbols into the clay—some chose intricate patterns, others left simple fingerprints. I read from Eph 2:10: "For we are God's handiwork, created in Christ Jesus to do good works, which God prepared in advance for us to do." "Think of this step as your own contribution to the work God is doing in your life," I said. "What marks will you leave behind as a reflection of your faith and your journey?" Some participants pressed rugged textures into their crosses to make them look aged. Others used organic motifs like vines or flowers. For a few, the act of decorating led to mistakes, requiring them to start over—an opportunity to reflect on grace and renewal as they wedged their clay and began again.

Contemplatio (Contemplation): Reflection and Blessing

When the crosses were complete, I asked everyone to sit quietly, holding their creations. I read from Ps 103: "For he knows how we are formed; he remembers that we are dust." "Take a moment," I said, "to reflect on this process. What have you learned about yourself, about God, or about the act of creation? Where have you encountered grace tonight?" The moment that followed was heavy with thought and prayer. Some participants closed their eyes, others traced the lines and patterns they had made. It was a sacred moment to recognize God's presence in the ordinary and the extraordinary alike.

Traditio (Offering): Releasing for Firing

Finally, we moved to the drying rack, where each person placed their cross to be fired later in the kiln. I read from Prov 16:3: "Commit to the Lord whatever you do, and he will establish your plans"; and from Heb 12:28–29: "Therefore, let us be thankful, and so worship God acceptably with reverence and awe, for our God is a consuming fire." "This step," I explained, "is about trust. You've shaped your cross, but now you must let it go. The kiln will transform it, just as God uses the refining trials of life to strengthen and reshape us. This is an act of surrender—of letting go and allowing God to complete the work."

As I stood in the studio that evening, watching participants carefully place their crosses on the drying rack, I was struck by how this simple act of making had opened a window to God's grace. The process of *fabricandi divina* wasn't just about crafting with clay—it was about being crafted ourselves, shaped and transformed by the loving hands of our Creator.

This practice encapsulates the work of this chapter: that making is not merely a metaphor for theological reflection but a means of encountering God. The act of creating—whether shaping a pot or pressing a cross from clay—opens us to the rhythms of formation and transformation that lie at the heart of the Christian life. By integrating the arts into theology—not just as objects to be admired but as practices to be lived—we expand the horizons of theological inquiry. The studio becomes not only a workshop but a sanctuary, where creativity meets faith and where the joy of making reveals the extraordinary God who shapes us all.

6

Theology, Culture, and the Environment

INTRODUCTION: A FLOODED LANDSCAPE

In April of 2019, I flew back to Omaha, Nebraska, to be with my dying father. From birth until late elementary school, I grew up on a family farm in southwest Iowa. My father came from a long line of farmers, and the land was as much a part of our family as any of its human members. Though Iowa and Nebraska are often disparagingly referred to as "flyover states," for me, they were home.

Having flown over the Midwest hundreds of times, I have never tired of looking out the window at the patchwork of fields. The quilt of green squares in Iowa slowly transitioned to the circular irrigation patterns as you traveled farther west into Colorado. Like an aerial tapestry, each piece represented someone's labor and livelihood. But on that April morning, as the plane descended toward Omaha's Eppley Airfield, the once-familiar landscape had been replaced by something alien: everything was a murky brown.

A once-in-a-generation flood had covered the Missouri River Valley in feet of water, from the Dakotas down to Missouri. Levees had burst their banks, and entire towns, crops, and livelihoods were swept away. Punctuating the desolate landscape were bright pops of yellow where corn silos had ruptured, the grain—last year's harvest—expanding as it absorbed the floodwaters and poured out the sides of ruined grain bins.

Since humans began planting crops, water management has been a part of farming. My father used to tell stories of a flood in the 1940s that brought water up to the second-story windows of the family farmhouse (though he was known to exaggerate, as fathers do!). In my own lifetime, I remember the flood of 1984, which brought the governor of Iowa and local TV crews from Omaha out to our farm to survey the damage. But none of these stories compared to the devastation of 2019—a disaster meteorologists attributed to anthropogenic climate change.

The small town nearest our family farm, Pacific Junction—no more than a stop on the railroad westward—was nearly destroyed. The Methodist church where my grandmother had worshiped for decades was washed away. There's a terrible irony here: the industrialized agriculture that fuels climate change also increases the vulnerability of farmers and their crops worldwide, putting their lives and livelihoods at even greater risk.

For many, connecting theology or everyday life with environmental concerns may seem unusual. Yet few things affect our daily lives more than the outcomes of our stewardship—or lack thereof—of the creation. The first creation story in Genesis reminds us that humans are not separate from creation; we are part of it, embedded in a complex web of relationships and entrusted with the care of the world we inhabit.

This chapter explores this theological vision of creation care, addressing historical critiques of Christianity's relationship with the environment and examining contemporary theological responses. We will consider environmentally focused movements that have arisen in response to this crisis and reflect on what it means to live faithfully in an age of climate change.

WHO'S TO BLAME?

For millennia, our agrarian ancestors understood their lives to be inextricably linked with the forces of nature. Ancient Near Eastern religions, from which and around which ancient Israelite religion emerged, developed elaborate stories to explain the vagaries and regularities of the seasons. The annual ebb and flow of the Nile were translated into tales of the divine cycles of life and death in Egyptian mythology, while epic floods like those described in the Gilgamesh Epic or the biblical Noahic myth reflected the unpredictable flood/drought cycle experienced by civilizations reliant on rivers like the Tigris or Euphrates (an experience not unlike my own family's relationship with the Missouri River). The Deuteronomic law connects covenantal faithfulness with the fertility of the land (Deut 28:1–6), while famine, flood, and pestilence are framed as consequences of corporate sin (Deut 28:15, 23–24). The import of the natural world is further reflected in the prophetic imagination of Hosea, for whom the "spring rains" that would have come from the cool western winds off of the Mediterranean were seen as a sign of divine blessing and renewal (Hos 6:3), while the harsh and arid winds from the east portended divine judgment (Hos 13:15).

In industrialized and urbanized nations, the deep connection between persons, communities, and the environment seems broken, and the meaning that previous generations drew from the creation appears dulled. How did we arrive here, and is there a deeper theological root to the environmental degradation we now witness?

THE WHITE THESIS AND CHRISTIANITY'S ROLE IN ENVIRONMENTAL DEGRADATION

One popular attempt to identify the causes of environmental degradation came from Lynn White, an influential American professor of medieval history. In a highly controversial article entitled "The Historical Roots of Our Ecological Crisis" published in 1967 in the journal *Nature*, White argues that Christian thought, with its anthropocentrism and instrumental view of nature, created the ideological and theological foundation for the West's environmental crisis. White argues that in contrast to the cyclical views of history and sacred vision of nature that were held by pre-Christian pagan religions, Christianity asserted a definite beginning and end to world history and a dominative perspective over nature that demonized the historical and natural worlds in light of the world to come. The new relationship to nature and history imposed by the ethos of Christian Europe viewed nature as an object that could be made to serve ends that originated from societal and religious goals rather than ends that originated within nature itself. White notes that in response to the view of sacred nature advanced by paganism, Christian theology exorcised the animating spirits of the natural world:

> To a Christian a tree can be no more than a physical fact. The whole concept of the sacred grove is alien to Christianity and to the ethos of the West. For nearly two millennia Christian missionaries have been chopping down sacred groves, which are idolatrous because they assume spirit in nature.[1]

1. White, "Historical Roots," 1206.

In a nature denuded of its sacred import, Christian Europeans were free to explore and exploit the natural world with the intent of pursuing further means of exerting "dominion over nature," all with the ends of the kingdom of God in mind. The long-lasting result of this theological disposition toward nature, as argued by White, has been the exploitation of the natural world by the processes of industrialization in the West. Had Christianity not believed that it was at the pinnacle of the natural order—as informed by a literal reading of Gen 1:28 and Ps 8:5—White argued that our ecological situation would be very different indeed.

The argument advanced by White suggests that the way in which nature was "viewed" by Christian Europe encouraged exploitative practices. A similar position was expressed by the German philosopher Martin Heidegger (1889–1976) in his famous essay "The Question Concerning Technology" (1954). Heidegger believed that modern technology had the effect of changing the way that we view the natural world. Nature, within such a modern technological milieu, is thwarted from its ability to function as an unmediated source of revealing. As his example, Heidegger examines the means by which contemporary technology takes hold of the natural world for the production of energy. Whereas the ancient modes of deriving energy were anchored to the underlying forces of nature, modern technology grasps hold of (en-frames) nature and compels it to submit to humanity's needs. Heidegger reflected on how a hydroelectric dam challenges the status of a river as an aesthetic or natural object and reduces it to a means of deriving electrical power. The scenario is much the same for the production of coal-fired electricity:

> A tract of land is challenged in the hauling out of coal and ore. The earth now reveals itself as a coal mining district, the soil as a mineral deposit. The field that the peasant formerly cultivated and set in order appears differently than it did when to set in order still meant to take care of and maintain.[2]

As a metaphor for the modern engagement with the environment, coal-fueled power stations show how modern technology forcibly draws from nature a foreign and imposed end (the extraction of energy), removing from nature what Heidegger would see as nature's natural ends (a beautiful field that reveals something of nature to the one who views

---

2. Heidegger, "Question Concerning Technology," 320.

it).³ As such, nature is revealed as a "standing-reserve," and for Heidegger, "whatever stands by in the sense of standing-reserve no longer stands over against us as object."⁴ Thus, the most dangerous impact of modern technology is not the exploitation of nature, as such, but the detrimental changes made to human perception as a result of technological thinking.⁵

Reexamining the "White Thesis"

White was a historian, and his argument was principally focused on the historical roots, not the contemporary causes, of the environmental crisis. In fact, even though White blames certain elements of Christian thought (anthropocentrism, primarily) for creating a context in which nature could be exploited, he concludes his article by appealing to religion as a potential resource for challenging such exploitative practices. In particular, he calls for Christians to emulate the life of St. Francis of Assisi, who White suggests should become the patron saint of ecologists! He urges people of all faiths, but Christians in particular, to live in harmony with the natural world and to view nature as a gift from God that should be cherished and managed wisely.

It is doubtful that White could have imagined the wide reception of his article. Despite the intentionally historical nature of his research, it spurred on an exhaustive study of religion and environmentalism by sociologists of religion and theologians alike.⁶ Following the publication of White's essay, many theologians and Christian leaders recognized the need to respond to the allegation that Christianity was inherently antienvironmental. While White's thesis suggested that Christianity contributed to ecological exploitation, subsequent theological work sought to reclaim the biblical tradition as a foundation for environmental care. Far from being a faith tradition of dominion and exploitation, Christian theology, when properly understood, promotes the protection and stewardship of creation.⁷

---

3. Heidegger, "Question Concerning Technology," 321.
4. Heidegger, "Question Concerning Technology," 322.
5. Heidegger, "Question Concerning Technology," 329.
6. DeLashmutt, "Church and Climate Change."
7. John Black (*Dominion of Man* [1970]), Barbour (*Technology, Environment* [1980]), and Attfield (*Ethics of Environmental Concern* [1983]) were early figures in raising the environmental awareness of Christians, and work in this field has continued in several other pro-environmental Christian theological and ethical volumes, e.g., Moltmann, *God in Creation* (1985); McFague, *Body of God* (1993); Northcott, *Environment and Christian Ethics* (1996); Deane-Drummond, *Theology and Ecology* (1996); *Eco-Theology*

THE BIBLE AND THE DOCTRINE OF CREATION

The why of a Christian environmental ethic is grounded in the doctrine of creation—a doctrine that not only speaks of the origins of the universe but also forms the foundation for understanding God's relationship to the world and humanity's role within it. This means that the environmental challenges we face—climate change, deforestation, species extinction, and pollution—are more than issues of resource management but deeply theological concerns. They challenge us to ask: How do we, as Christians, live faithfully in a world groaning under the weight of ecological degradation?

The biblical narrative offers a multifaceted understanding of creation, woven throughout various genres of Scripture—narrative, poetry, prophecy, and wisdom literature. The foundation of this theology is laid in the opening chapters of Genesis, where two distinct creation accounts set the tone for the entire biblical witness on creation. As noted in a previous chapter, in Gen 1, creation unfolds as a highly structured and ordered process. The narrative presents a cosmic view of creation, with God speaking the world into existence over six days, culminating in the Sabbath. In this account, the emphasis is on the power of God's word to bring order out of chaos. God's creation is systematic, with each day following a rhythm of divine command, creation, and evaluation, as God declares each part of creation "good."

The Gen 2 account, by contrast, offers a more intimate and anthropocentric vision of creation. Here, God forms Adam from the dust of the ground and breathes life into him, emphasizing the relational aspect between God and humanity. While Gen 1 portrays creation as a cosmic event, Gen 2 focuses on the creation of humans and their role within creation, including the establishment of human relationships and responsibility for the

---

(2008); Bouma-Prediger, *For the Beauty of the Earth* (2001); Berry, *God's Book of Works* (2003); Spencer and White, *Christianity, Climate Change* (2007); Atkinson, *Renewing the Face of the Earth* (2008); Jenkins, *Ecologies of Grace* (2008). More recently, much writing on theology and the environment has attempted to address the particular dangers posed both by anthropogenic climate change and by the tendency for those associated with the religious right to politicize and deny the risks of climate change, e.g., Hughes et al., *Ecological Solidarities* (2019); Jorgenson and Padget, *Ecotheology* (2020); Cole and Walker, *Theology on a Defiant Earth* (2022); Marlow and Harris, *Bible and Ecology* (2022); Van Montfoort, *Green Theology* (2022); Antal, *Climate Church, Climate World* (2023); Northcott, *God and Gaia* (2023); Quinsey, *Christian Environmentalism* (2023); Joranko, "Engaging the Climate Crisis" (2024). Collectively, their works offer an important apologetic for the importance of Christian involvement in pro-environmental actions, showing that it is deeply and historically Christian to be concerned for the welfare of creation.

creation. These two narratives complement one another by offering both a macrocosmic and microcosmic view of creation—God is both the cosmic Creator and the personal God who forms and sustains life.

Theologically, these two accounts affirm several important points about creation: creation is ordered, good, and intentional. Humanity, created in the image of God, is given a unique role in tending and caring for creation, a theme that will resurface throughout Scripture. Furthermore, the Sabbath's centrality in Gen 1 highlights the importance of rest and worship, connecting creation with the rhythm of divine and human life.

The prophetic literature of the Hebrew Bible deepens the theological understanding of creation by connecting it to God's covenant with Israel and God's salvific work. In passages such as Isa 51:9–11 and 65:17–18, creation is portrayed not only as a past event but as an ongoing process that culminates in God's promise of a new heaven and new earth. The prophetic vision of new creation extends beyond the world we see to encompass the restoration of Israel and the renewal of the entire cosmos.

The psalms and wisdom literature celebrate creation as a reflection of God's goodness, beauty, and order. Psalms 8, 19, and 104 speak to the majesty of creation, declaring that the cosmos reflects the glory and handiwork of God. The psalms also highlight the role of creation in worship. In Ps 145:5, creation itself is depicted as a springboard for human praise, inviting all creatures to join in the worship of their Creator. The wisdom tradition further explores the relationship between creation and divine order. Proverbs 8 personifies wisdom as being present at creation, working alongside God to bring the world into existence. Wisdom represents the intelligibility and order of the world, affirming that creation is not random but reflects divine purpose and design. The book of Job also reflects on creation, particularly in God's speeches (Job 38–41), where creation is presented as an awe-inspiring, yet ultimately mysterious, manifestation of divine wisdom and power.

The New Testament adds the theme of creation by presenting Jesus Christ as central to the cosmic order. In John 1, Christ is identified as the divine Logos, the one through whom all things were made. This reflects the idea that Christ, as the preexistent Word, is the agent of creation, working alongside the Father and the Spirit. Colossians 1:15–17 echoes this theme, declaring that "in him all things were created" and that Christ is the one who holds all things together. And, as was the case in Old Testament prophetic language, the New Testament continues to affirm the link between

God's act in creating and God's work of redeeming. Passages like 2 Cor 5:17 and Rev 21:1 point to the unique role of Christ in bringing about a "new creation," suggesting that just as Christ was present in the first creation, he is faithful to also bring about the renewal of all things in the eschatological future.

The biblical witness, with its rich imagery of creation, challenges us to see the world not as something to be exploited but as a reflection of God's goodness, a place where God's Spirit dwells and works. Moreover, creation theology invites us to a deeper understanding of worship. As we praise God for the gift of creation, we are reminded of our role as stewards and co-creators, tasked with nurturing and protecting the earth. In reclaiming the richness of creation theology, we also reclaim our responsibility as people of faith to care for the world that God has made, to seek justice for all living things, and to work toward the flourishing of all creation in harmony with our Creator.

A THEOLOGY OF HOPE IN AN AGE OF ECOLOGICAL DESPAIR

Christian ecotheology is as diverse as the traditions within Christianity itself, offering a mosaic of responses to the environmental crisis. Laurel Kearns has categorized these responses into three major streams: the Christian stewardship ethic, the eco-justice ethic, and creation spirituality.[8] Each framework reflects a unique theological lens, yet all converge in their recognition of the urgent need for faithful engagement with creation.

Christian Stewardship Ethic

The Christian stewardship ethic, familiar to many Evangelicals and conservative Christians, is deeply rooted in biblical imagery. This framework sees humanity as caretakers of the earth, entrusted with its well-being by divine mandate. Drawing from Gen 2:15, where Adam is called to "work and keep" the garden, this ethic emphasizes humanity's role in reflecting God's image through the care and cultivation of creation.

Stewardship theology underscores the transcendent nature of God, asserting that the earth belongs to God and that humanity's role is one

---

8. Kearns, "Saving the Creation."

of responsible oversight. Environmental degradation is viewed as a result of human sinfulness, and the path to restoration lies in repentance, reestablishing right relationships with God, and embracing biblically guided environmental practices.

Prominent figures such as Calvin DeWitt, Wendell Berry, and Loren Wilkinson have championed this ethic, advocating for a holistic stewardship that encompasses reverence for creation as an integral part of Christian discipleship. Stewardship here is not mere conservation; it is a covenantal response to God's call, affirming the sacredness of all life.

Eco-Justice Ethic

The eco-justice ethic moves beyond individual responsibility, addressing systemic inequities that exacerbate environmental degradation. This framework highlights the interconnectedness of ecological and social justice, recognizing that environmental harm disproportionately affects the poor and marginalized.

Rooted in liberation theology, eco-justice theology extends the biblical mandate to care for "the least of these" (Matt 25:40) to include the earth itself. The suffering of creation and vulnerable populations are seen as inseparable, calling Christians to act in solidarity with the oppressed—both human and nonhuman.

Theologians such as Leonardo Boff, Sallie McFague, and Larry Rasmussen emphasize that environmental justice requires systemic change. This ethic challenges Christians to confront the economic and political forces driving ecological destruction, integrating christological themes of justice and liberation into environmental action.

Creation Spirituality

Creation spirituality offers a mystical and holistic approach, emphasizing the sacredness of all creation and humanity's spiritual interconnectedness with the earth. This perspective often draws from panentheistic or even pantheistic views, seeing God as intimately present in the fabric of the cosmos.

Advocates like Thomas Berry, Matthew Fox, and Joanna Macy argue that humanity's alienation from nature lies at the heart of the ecological crisis. Their solution lies in rediscovering a profound spiritual connection to creation, fostering practices such as eco-liturgy, meditation, and nature-based rituals that celebrate the earth's sanctity.

Creation spirituality calls Christians to move beyond seeing the environment as a resource to be managed. Instead, it invites a reverent encounter with creation as a sacred reality, reflecting the divine presence.

The Anglican Perspective: Safeguarding Creation

Anglican ecotheology embodies elements of all three models, weaving them into a cohesive vision of creation care. The Anglican Communion's engagement with environmental issues began formally at the 1968 Lambeth Conference, where bishops called for responsible stewardship and the prevention of pollution. This commitment evolved into the fifth Mark of Mission in the 1980s: "To strive to safeguard the integrity of creation, and sustain and renew the life of the earth."[9]

Institutional initiatives such as the Anglican Environment Network (AEN) have bolstered cross-Communion collaboration, encouraging grassroots and global efforts. Programs like the "Shrinking the Footprint" campaign demonstrate a practical commitment to reducing the church's carbon footprint, integrating environmental ethics into everyday practice.

Anglican theologians, including John Habgood and Michael Northcott, have enriched ecotheological discourse. Their works explore themes of sacramental creation, global justice, and the intersection of eschatology and climate ethics, offering a distinctively Anglican response to the ecological crisis.

The Anglican tradition also emphasizes worship and liturgy as vehicles for creation care. Observances like the season of creation incorporate prayers and rituals that celebrate the earth, reminding Christians of their spiritual and ethical responsibility to care for it.

Contemporary Environmental Theologies

In the past decade, ecotheology has not only maintained its relevance but also deepened and evolved in response to the pressing realities of climate change. One significant shift has been the growing awareness of the acute and existential threats posed by climate change. While earlier theological

---

9. Anglican Communion, "Marks of Mission."

engagements, particularly in the late 1990s and early 2000s, recognized environmental degradation as a moral issue, the threat of climate change was often considered more theoretical. Today, however, the direct and catastrophic impacts of climate change are undeniable and immediate. We are no longer debating potential outcomes but witnessing real-time consequences—rising sea levels, superstorms, wildfires, and climate refugees, among others.

The growing inclusion of non-Western voices in theological discourse has also enriched Christian environmental thought. There is now greater awareness of how indigenous spiritualities and non-Christian traditions view creation, offering valuable resources for addressing the climate crisis. This emerging trend reflects a shift away from the Western-dominated narrative that has, historically, contributed to ecological exploitation. In the spirit of Lynn White's critique, which linked Western industrialization with environmental destruction, theologians and ethicists now recognize that solutions may well lie in engaging with non-Western cosmologies and practices that emphasize harmony with nature rather than domination over it.

A third key development is the increasing focus on the intersection of environmental care and social justice. Earlier forms of ecotheology, particularly within deep ecology and ecospirituality, often concentrated on the moral dimensions of environmental degradation as it primarily affected nonhuman creation. However, contemporary ecotheology emphasizes the interconnectedness of ecological destruction and human suffering. As environmental harms have worsened, it has become clear that the most vulnerable human populations—often in the Global South—bear the brunt of climate change. For example, communities in low-lying countries like Bangladesh face ongoing threats from rising sea levels and extreme weather, illustrating how environmental degradation and social inequality are inextricably linked.

Christian theology now understands environmental care not merely as an issue of creation care but as a broader matter of justice. We must recognize that our consumer choices have far-reaching impacts—affecting not only ecosystems but also the lives of people we may never meet on the other side of the planet. The ethic of creation care calls Christians to love God by loving the world God made, recognizing its intrinsic value and protecting its integrity. At the same time, we are called to love our neighbors, understanding that how we interact with creation directly impacts the well-being of others.

CHRISTIAN THEOLOGY: A FRAMEWORK FOR CLIMATE CARE

As we seek to frame an ethic of climate care, we might appeal to something akin to the fundamentals of Christian ethics: love of God and love of neighbor. This dual commandment provides the foundation for how Christians might understand their responsibility to the environment. To this end, we express our love of God when we care for the creation that God has given us. In Scripture, creation is depicted as a divine gift—an act of free love from a God who chose to create something other than God's self out of the abundance of love that eternally flows between the persons of the Trinity. This act of creation is not a one-time event but part of an ongoing relationship between God and the cosmos, one in which humans are called to participate.

Christopher Southgate reminds us that, within the vast scope of creation, the time allotted to humanity is infinitesimally small. In his theological reflections, Southgate emphasizes the cosmic scale of creation, which spans billions of years and includes not only human history but the life of countless species, ecosystems, and processes that have existed long before humans and will continue long after. His work invites us to reconsider our place in creation, humbling us with the awareness that we are a brief moment in an ongoing cosmic narrative. As Southgate notes, the created world does not exist solely for human benefit, and yet, as humans, we are uniquely capable of reflecting on this vast narrative and responding to it in awe and worship.[10]

Scripture also frames creation as an active participant in the worship of God, with humans being enjoined to join creation in this sacred task. Psalm 19 reads, "The heavens declare the glory of God," and the New Testament reveals how even the stones would cry out in praise if humans were silent (Luke 19:40). This framing suggests that human participation in creation's flourishing is also an act of worship. When we translate our awe and gratitude for the beauty and complexity of the world into worship of the Creator, we engage in a profound theological practice. Thus, when Christians act as wise stewards of creation—whether through symbolic actions like recycling, or individual efforts to reduce carbon emissions, or larger efforts to prevent the extinction of endangered species and protect habitats—these actions are expressions of our love for God. We love God by caring for and protecting the beautiful world God has given us.

---

10. Southgate, *God, Humanity and the Cosmos*, 179.

On the other hand, the Christian ethic of neighborly love compels us to consider how our environmental practices—whether related to consumption, production, or energy extraction—affect the lives of those around us. In our modern, globalized world, we must recognize that the consequences of our actions are not confined to our immediate surroundings. Rather, they reverberate across ecosystems and impact communities far beyond our sight. As theologians like Michael Northcott have argued, we must expand our understanding of "neighbor" to include both human and nonhuman neighbors. This broader definition compels us to think critically about how our environmental actions—whether they degrade land, contribute to climate change, or exploit natural resources—harm not just animals and ecosystems but also the livelihoods of countless humans around the globe.[11]

Even if we do not fully adopt cosmologies that lean toward panpsychism or the Gaia hypothesis, we must still acknowledge that our actions have profound ecological and human consequences. For example, the carbon emissions produced in industrialized nations contribute to rising sea levels that threaten the homes of millions in coastal regions like Bangladesh. These communities, whose languages we may never know and whose faces we may never see, are directly harmed by our environmental practices. Therefore, a Christian environmental ethic must be keenly aware of the interconnectedness of human and ecological well-being. Our commitment to neighborly love should extend to all those affected by our actions, including those living in distant parts of the world, whose lives and livelihoods are shaped by the environmental choices we make. This ethic requires us to act not just for the sake of creation itself but for the countless neighbors—human and nonhuman—whose flourishing is intertwined with the health of the planet.

HOW THE CHURCH CAN MAKE A DIFFERENCE

In this context of ecological despair, the church is uniquely positioned to offer hope and foster change. While symbolic actions such as recycling programs and the reduction of carbon footprints are valuable, the church's role extends beyond these gestures to influence systemic change through investments, education, and advocacy.

---

11. Northcott, "Ecology and Christian Ethics."

Investment: The church holds significant financial power through its investments. By divesting from industries that contribute to environmental degradation, particularly fossil fuels, and instead investing in sustainable and regenerative industries, the church can help shift economic systems toward greener practices. As abby mohaupt's work on the Presbyterian Church (USA) shows, divestment is not only a symbolic act but also a powerful statement of the church's values and a means of leveraging financial resources for ecological justice.[12]

Education: The church has the ability to create counternarratives that challenge the consumer-driven ethos of immediate gratification. By educating parishioners about the theological significance of creation and encouraging a culture of environmental responsibility, the church can cultivate a community that understands the importance of living in harmony with the earth. This education extends to understanding our role within the interconnected web of life, where our actions affect both the environment and our fellow humans.

Advocacy: The church can mobilize its large and diverse communities to advocate for policies that address the root causes of climate change. By using its voice to influence policymakers and corporations, the church can play a pivotal role in pushing for structural changes that promote sustainability and justice on a global scale. Advocacy, as shown in works like Joranko's reflections on spiritual nonviolence, demonstrates how the church can model active resistance to environmental degradation while fostering community resilience and solidarity.[13]

It is challenging to remain hopeful in an age of superstorms, rising sea levels, and climate refugees. At times, it feels as though more energy is being spent on dreams of colonizing Mars or escaping Earth than on caring for the only planet we have. The narratives of doom and destruction are overwhelming, and yet, as Christians, we are called to hope. This hope is not naive or blind to the reality of the environmental crisis, but it is grounded in the knowledge that God is still at work in the world, sustaining creation and moving it toward its ultimate fulfillment. The theology of hope that Christians bring to the table is one that is grounded in the belief that God is still at work in creation, sustaining it even amid crisis. While the damage caused by climate change may seem insurmountable, Christian hope rests in the eschatological promise of renewal. This hope calls the

---

12. mohaupt, "Corporate Confession."
13. Joranko, "Engaging the Climate Crisis."

SECTION 2: LOCATIONS OF MEANING MAKING

church not to passive waiting but to active engagement, working for the healing of creation while trusting in God's ultimate plan for restoration.

Section 3
Theology at Work and Play

7

A Theology of Work

"MY NAME IS MICHAEL, AND I'M A WORKAHOLIC."

I HAVE HAD A career-long interest in how theology intersects with work. I've given presentations on the gift of administration, published articles exploring the spiritual lives of technology workers, led discussions on organizational discernment, and recently completed a major research-based study on executive leadership transitions in theological education.

I often say that theology is, in no small part, autobiography. As I reflect on my own focus on "work," I realize it stems from a lifelong wrestle with an unhealthy relationship to work—something that could easily be called workaholism.

Like many struggles, this likely began in childhood, shaped by what I saw modeled by my father. My dad worked extraordinary hours. He'd rise at 5:00 a.m., head to the farm to give the hands their tasks for the day, then stop at the café in town to meet friends—who were often clients and partners in his other ventures—before heading to the John Deere dealership. In the evenings, after coming home to shower and clean up, he'd attend networking events like Rotary meetings or similar gatherings. He rarely took time off, even on weekends and holidays. Family vacations were infrequent, and when we did go somewhere, he would call in to work every morning and evening to ensure everything was running smoothly. Even when he was actively dying of cancer from 2018 to 2019, he continued to work daily until entering hospice. The last time I saw my father alive was at his desk in the insurance office he ran in our hometown, just a month before his death.

SECTION 3: THEOLOGY AT WORK AND PLAY

This dedication to work was deeply ingrained in me, though I'm not particularly proud of it. My first job after college, working in the dot-com sector in Seattle in the late 1990s, found me working ungodly hours—once spending two weeks sleeping under my desk during a particularly tense period of coding while rolling out a new platform. During the five years I attended seminary part-time, I juggled seventy-plus-hour weeks at Allrecipes.com, night classes at Fuller's extension campus in Seattle, and active responsibilities at a church where I preached, taught Sunday school, and helped with pastoral duties for a congregation of more than two hundred people. My days regularly began before dawn and ended near midnight.

Work in America Today

Kassandra Vaughn provocatively begins an article in Medium with the following quote:

> 1/3 of your life will be spent at work.
> That's 90,000 hours over the course of a lifetime.
> The average American spends over 100 hours commuting.
> By the age of 30, most people will have had 7 or 8 jobs.
> 80% of workers hate their jobs.
> Oh, and couples where one partner spends 10+ hours more than usual at work divorce at twice the average rate (we're already above the 50% divorce rate).
> Can you see where this is going?
> And here's the real question:
> Are you happy at the one place you are spending most of your life?
> For most people, the answer is No.
> So here's the next question:
> Why are so many people choosing to live like this?
> Because they don't believe they have the capacity, ability, and time to do something else.[1]

Vaughn accurately identifies a problem many of us can relate to. However, rather than critiquing work itself, she suggests that finding happiness requires taking "ownership" and "action" so you can "get to where you want to go" and "NEVER AGAIN put [your] future in the hands of ONE person who can ruin your life."[2]

---

1. K. Vaughn, "90,000 Hours," opening lines.
2. K. Vaughn, "90,000 Hours," steps 1, 5, 4, 10.

Effectively, her solution to spending one-third of life at work is ensuring you like what you do—echoing the old adage "Love what you do, and you'll never work a day in your life." But is this enough?

What Is Work?

Generally speaking, work can be understood as having two primary components: intrinsic motivation (the enjoyment or fulfillment derived from work) and extrinsic motivation (work as a necessity for survival—"if you don't work, you don't eat"). The problem with advice like Vaughn's, which places the onus on the worker to find fulfillment in their work, is that it overlooks the vast majority of workers—both historically and globally—whose jobs offer little intrinsic value and serve purely as a means to support themselves or their families.

A recent article by Emily Batdorf in *Forbes* highlights that providing for daily needs is what motivates most American workers. A 2023 survey conducted by Payroll.org found that 78 percent of Americans live paycheck to paycheck, a 6 percent increase from the previous year. This means that more than three-quarters of Americans struggle to save or invest after covering their monthly expenses.

Similarly, a 2023 Forbes Advisor survey revealed that nearly 70 percent of respondents either identified as living paycheck to paycheck (40 percent) or, even more concerningly, reported that their income doesn't cover their standard expenses (29 percent).[3]

While not everyone in this group works purely for the money, the widespread difficulty of saving for retirement—much less accruing wealth—points to a systemic issue with our approach to work. For example, nearly nine million workers in the United States hold multiple jobs (5.3 percent of the civilian workforce), according to a report by Jennifer Nash.[4]

Gallup's *State of the Global Workplace* 2024 report underscores several troubling trends that compound these challenges for workers worldwide:

- High stress levels persist, with 41 percent of employees reporting significant stress, and actively disengaged employees experiencing even greater stress than the unemployed.[5]

---

3. Batdorf, "Living Paycheck to Paycheck."
4. Nash, "Multiple Jobholders."
5. Gallup, *State of the Global Workplace*, 1.

- Daily loneliness affects 20 percent of employees, with remote workers particularly vulnerable (25 percent) compared to on-site workers (16 percent).[6]
- Younger employees' well-being has declined, reversing a historical trend where younger generations rated their lives more positively than older ones.[7]
- Poor management practices are a significant factor, correlating with increased stress, sadness, and loneliness. Managers themselves report higher stress levels than their nonmanagerial counterparts.[8]
- Despite strong labor protections in some regions, gaps in enforcement leave many employees exposed to unfair or unsafe conditions.[9]

Global employee engagement also stagnated in 2023, failing to build on prior improvements. Additionally, many workers report struggles with work-life balance—some cite an inability to attend family events, while others feel constantly exhausted by their workload.[10] Organizational responses, such as well-being apps, are often perceived as superficial and can worsen dissatisfaction when they fail to address the deeper, structural issues.[11]

These findings indicate the urgent need for systemic changes in how we structure and manage work. Without such changes, workplace stress, disengagement, and dissatisfaction will continue to undermine human flourishing. All of this leads me to ask a question that is central to this book: Where's God in this? Or more specifically, what does our theological understanding of humanity—and more specifically, human flourishing—reveal about our relationship with work? Is the issue with work a reflection of our choices, or does it stem from deeper structural or theological problems? How might the doctrine of creation (protology) reveal God's original intent for labor, of eschatology shape our hope for its ultimate purpose, and of pneumatology sustain us in the present tensions? Furthermore, is there an alternative to work that better captures what it means to be human and flourish in God's design? These questions frame the journey ahead in this chapter.

---

6. Gallup, *State of the Global Workplace*, 6.
7. Gallup, *State of the Global Workplace*, 7.
8. Gallup, *State of the Global Workplace*, 1, 18.
9. Gallup, *State of the Global Workplace*, 3, 11.
10. Gallup, *State of the Global Workplace*, 14.
11. Gallup, *State of the Global Workplace*, 1.

A THEOLOGY OF WORK: THE REFORMATION LEGACY[12]

The Reformation era reshaped many dimensions of Christian life, not least of which was the understanding of work and vocation. Martin Luther and John Calvin introduced theological frameworks that dismantled medieval notions of labor as a hierarchical dichotomy between the sacred and the secular. In doing so, they laid the groundwork for what Max Weber would later term the "Protestant work ethic," a cultural force that has left an indelible imprint on Western society, including the economic ethos of the United States. Their theological insights continue to provoke and inspire contemporary discussions on the meaning of work.

Luther: Work as Worship and Service

For Martin Luther, work was fundamentally reimagined as a divine calling, a sacred endeavor shared by all believers. Rejecting the medieval stratification that elevated monastic life as uniquely holy, Luther emphasized the universal priesthood of all believers. In his view, every vocation—from the farmer in the field to the homemaker scrubbing floors—held the potential to glorify God when approached in faith and love. This democratization of work invited Christians to see their daily labor as not only necessary but sacred.

Luther's reframing of vocation shifted the focus of labor from self-salvation to service. Grounded in his theology of grace, work was not a means to earn divine favor but a response to it. For Luther, labor became an expression of love for one's neighbor, a tangible way to participate in God's ongoing provision for the world. This integration of faith and works resonated deeply, shaping the cultural ethos of diligence, responsibility, and industriousness that came to define the Protestant work ethic.

Yet, Luther's theology of work was not merely theological; it carried profound cultural and economic implications. By sanctifying the ordinary, Luther empowered communities to embrace labor with a renewed sense of dignity and purpose. His influence extended far beyond the church, catalyzing a moral framework in which productivity and responsibility became virtues deeply embedded in societal structures.

---

12. Sarto, "Trabajo en Martín Lutero"; Capps and Carlin, "Releasing Life's Potential"; Cosden, "Work and the New Creation"; Richmann, "About Vocation"; Theology of Work Project, "Calling."

Calvin: Discipline and Divine Purpose

John Calvin built on Luther's foundation, weaving work into his broader theological vision of God's sovereignty and human purpose. For Calvin, work was inextricably tied to divine election. He envisioned labor as a response to God's calling, an act of worship that glorified the Creator. Each individual, Calvin argued, was endowed with unique gifts and a specific calling (*vocatio*), enabling them to contribute to the flourishing of creation in their particular sphere of influence.

Calvin's theology of work brought a unique emphasis on discipline. Work was not merely a necessity but a moral obligation, a disciplined practice that reflected both spiritual maturity and communal harmony. He also stressed the economic dimensions of work, encouraging thrift and reinvestment, practices that became hallmarks of the capitalist economies that emerged in Calvinist-influenced societies.

By embedding work within the context of divine providence, Calvin infused labor with an eternal significance. This perspective not only elevated the role of work but also framed it as a meaningful and disciplined response to God's sovereign will.[13]

From Theology to Culture: The Protestant Work Ethic

The theological insights of Luther and Calvin coalesced into a cultural phenomenon: the Protestant work ethic. Hard work became a moral imperative, and idleness was viewed as a vice. In societies influenced by these theological currents, work was not merely about survival but about fulfilling one's God-given purpose. This ethos shaped Western culture, particularly in the United States, where the values of self-reliance and industriousness were woven into the national identity.

Charles Taylor's notion of the rise of a disciplinary society offers a compelling lens through which to view the long-term implications of the Protestant work ethic. Taylor argues that the Reformation's desacralization of certain vocations (monastics, priests, etc.), alongside the sanctification of secular labor, reoriented Western society away from a more "enchanted" view of human life and agency. In this new framework, work acquired a

---

13. Stone, "John Calvin, the Work Ethic."

moral weight that replaced earlier understandings of divine providence and mystery with a more pragmatic, individualistic ethos.[14]

While this shift democratized work, infusing it with dignity and purpose, it also contributed to a cultural logic of productivity that prioritizes efficiency over contemplation. Taylor suggests that the loss of an enchanted worldview, one in which labor was embedded in a broader cosmic and sacramental order, has led to an increasingly utilitarian approach to human activity. Work, in this sense, became less about participation in God's providential care and more about the disciplined fulfillment of personal and societal goals.

This disciplinary ethos persists in contemporary culture, where the pressure to achieve, produce, and excel often eclipses the theological insights that first gave labor its dignity. Overwork and burnout have become hallmarks of modern life, revealing the tensions within this legacy. While theologians like Luther and Calvin emphasized work as a response to divine grace and a service to neighbor, the cultural forces they helped to unleash have, at times, distorted this vision, reducing work to a means of self-validation or economic survival.

Today, theologians wrestle with these tensions, seeking to recover a holistic vision of work that integrates meaningful labor with the Sabbath rhythms of rest and restoration. Taylor's analysis reminds us of the need to resist the disenchanted frameworks that dominate contemporary life and to reclaim a sense of wonder, humility, and sacredness in our vocations. By revisiting the theological roots of the Protestant work ethic, Christians can challenge the idolization of work and reimagine labor as a space for worship, community, and flourishing within the context of God's ongoing creation.

A THEOLOGY OF WORK: CREATION, REDEMPTION, AND THE SPIRIT'S ACTIVITY

One of the most significant modern contributors to the theology of work is Miroslav Volf, whose *Work in the Spirit* offers a deeply nuanced framework for understanding work as both a divine and human vocation. Volf situates work within three theological dimensions: protology (the doctrine of creation), eschatology (the doctrine of new creation), and pneumatology (the activity of the Holy Spirit). Through this lens, he reconciles the intrinsic

---

14. Taylor, *Secular Age*.

value of work with its redemptive purpose in God's transformative plans, advancing a vision of labor as a vital and cooperative act with God.[15]

Work in Protology: Foundations in Creation

Volf begins with the doctrine of creation, emphasizing humanity's role as co-creators with God. The Genesis narrative portrays human labor as a response to divine provision—God provides rain and sustenance, and humans cultivate and steward creation. This dynamic partnership affirms the dignity and purpose of work, grounding it in the theological concept of the imago Dei. Just as God's creative act brought order from chaos, human labor shapes and organizes what already exists, reflecting divine creativity.

However, Volf critiques interpretations of work that limit its role to preservation or maintenance. While sustaining creation is essential, he argues that modern labor transforms the world, requiring a broader theological framework that extends beyond the protological to include eschatological renewal.

Work in Eschatology: Transformation and Continuity

Volf's eschatological vision provides a powerful reinterpretation of work's ultimate purpose. He contrasts two models of eschatology: the annihilationist view, which envisions the current world being destroyed and replaced, and the transformational view, which sees the present world redeemed and perfected. Volf adopts the latter, suggesting that human labor contributes to the "building materials" of the new creation. Noble endeavors—those reflecting truth, goodness, and beauty—are not lost but purified and integrated into God's glorified world.

This transformational perspective imbues work with eternal significance. It validates even the seemingly transient or overlooked contributions of labor, whether artistic expressions, caregiving, or acts of justice. In Volf's view, these efforts, no matter how small, are woven into God's redemptive purposes, carrying forward into the eschaton as part of the new creation.

---

15. What follows is based on Volf's summary of his position ("Work as Cooperation").

Work in Pneumatology: The Spirit's Empowering Presence

The pneumatological dimension bridges creation and new creation, emphasizing the Holy Spirit's active role in human labor. Volf reimagines work as a charismatic activity, where the Spirit equips individuals with gifts (*charisms*) not only for ministry within the church but also for work in the broader world. This understanding infuses labor with divine purpose, transforming it into an act of cooperation with God's ongoing mission.

The Spirit's work, as Volf observes, extends beyond the spiritual to include material and cultural realms. From Bezalel, the Spirit-filled craftsman of Exodus, to modern expressions of creativity and care, the Spirit animates human efforts toward justice, beauty, and renewal. Through the Spirit, human labor becomes proleptic—anticipating the fullness of God's kingdom while contributing to its partial realization in the present.

A Critique and a Charismatic Alternative

While Volf draws on traditional Protestant notions of vocation, particularly Luther's democratization of labor as a divine calling, he critiques their limitations. Luther's framework, tied to rigid social stations, struggles to adapt to the dynamic and fluid nature of modern work contexts. In response, Volf proposes a charismatic theology of work, where diverse and adaptable gifts empower individuals to navigate changing roles and opportunities without losing sight of God's purposes.

Theological Synthesis: Work as Divine Collaboration

Volf's theology of work offers a cohesive vision that integrates creation, redemption, and the Spirit's activity. He redefines work as participation in God's mission, affirming its dignity and purpose even in the mundane. Success, in this view, is not measured by material achievements but by alignment with God's transformative goals—acts of creativity, care, and justice that contribute to the eschatological vision of renewal. This framework also liberates individuals from rigid vocational structures, encouraging freedom and flexibility to explore diverse callings while maintaining fidelity to God's mission. By grounding work in protology, eschatology, and pneumatology, Volf transcends the dichotomy of sacred and secular, reimagining labor as a vital expression of faith and hope. Finally, Volf's contributions to the theology of work inspire a renewed understanding of labor as a cooperative act with God. By weaving together creation, redemption, and the Spirit's empowerment, he invites Christians to view their work—whether artistic, administrative, or agricultural—as a meaningful participation in God's ongoing transformation of the world. In this vision, work becomes not just a human endeavor but a foretaste of the kingdom to come.

A THEOLOGY OF WORK: FROM TENDING TO TOILING

While Miroslav Volf provides a compelling and theologically rich framework for understanding work as a divine and human vocation, his approach raises questions about the tension between the theological affirmation of labor and the lived realities of work in a fallen world. The biblical witness, while affirming work's potential as an expression of divine creativity and purpose, also resists idealizing it. Themes of toil, futility, and critique—woven throughout Scripture—challenge the notion that work is inherently good or universally redemptive. By examining these tensions, we can expand the theological conversation to include alternative perspectives, such as Jeremy Posadas's anti-work theology, which critiques the deep entanglement of labor with human identity and purpose.[16]

TENDING AND TOILING: WORK IN SCRIPTURE

The Genesis narrative lays the groundwork for much of the theological reflection on work, yet it does so in a way that underscores a fundamental tension between labor as divine partnership and labor as burden. Before the fall, human work is depicted as harmonious and creative. In Gen 2:15, Adam is placed in the garden "to till and to keep it," a description of work that is cooperative and aligned with God's purposes. This vision of tending portrays humanity as stewards of creation, reflecting the divine image in their role as co-creators. Many theological traditions have idealized this prelapsarian labor as a model for understanding work's intrinsic dignity and purpose.

However, Gen 3 introduces a stark contrast. Postlapsarian labor is no longer harmonious but fraught with difficulty. The curse of toil—"Cursed is the ground because of you; in toil you shall eat of it all the days of your life"

---

16. Posadas, "Refusal of Work."

(Gen 3:17)—transforms work into a site of struggle, futility, and alienation. This shift complicates pro-work theologies that conflate pre- and post-fall labor. The biblical text acknowledges work's potential for creativity and co-operation but also confronts its realities of hardship and estrangement. This foundational tension between harmonious and burdensome labor finds further expression in the broader biblical narrative, where specific instances like Bezalel's craftsmanship and the existential reflections in Ecclesiastes offer additional insights into the nature of work.

The Non-Normativity of Work in Scripture

While work is a recurring theme in Scripture, it is neither universally celebrated nor presented as a normative calling for all people. Instead, work is often depicted as situational and secondary to divine purposes. As discussed in a previous chapter, in the story of Bezalel (Exod 31:1–6), we encounter one of the rare instances in Scripture where an individual is explicitly called and equipped by the Spirit of God for a specific task. Bezalel's craftsmanship in constructing the tabernacle underscores the sacred potential of human labor, but such examples are exceptional rather than normative. Most biblical figures are not called to specific professions but to roles within God's overarching redemptive plan.

Perhaps more normative for work taken as a whole, Ecclesiastes offers a sobering critique of labor. The writer's lament—"What do mortals gain from all the toil at which they toil under the sun?" (Eccl 1:3)—emphasizes the fleeting and often futile nature of human work. The vanity of labor, described in Eccl 2:18–23, suggests that work, while necessary, often fails to provide ultimate meaning or fulfillment. This critique challenges any theology that equates work with eternal value or ultimate purpose, urging a recognition of work's limitations in the broader scope of human existence.

Work and the Kingdom: Jesus' Reorientation

The life and teachings of Jesus reframe work within the context of God's kingdom, radically re-prioritizing labor in light of eternal values. Jesus himself models a departure from work-centric visions of life. Leaving behind his assumed carpentry trade, he calls his disciples to abandon their professions and follow him. The scene of fishermen leaving their nets in Matt 4:18–22 and the radical call to discipleship in Luke 14:26–27—where

Jesus demands leaving behind even family obligations—signal a redefinition of human priorities. In addition to re-prioritizing work in light of the kingdom, Jesus' emphasis on Sabbath rest and his critiques of wealth challenge the centrality of labor as a source of identity or security, inviting his followers to trust in God's provision.

Additionally, Jesus' teachings on earthly and heavenly treasures (Matt 6:19–21) highlight the temporal nature of material pursuits. By prioritizing the kingdom of God, the New Testament community redefined success, placing eternal values above economic achievements or societal norms. Work, while acknowledged, was never the defining marker of identity or purpose; it was always secondary to the mission of the church.

Subordinating Work in the Early Church

In Acts, the story that the church tells of its own origins, work was de-centered and placed within a broader framework of communal care and mission. While jobs like tent making and fishing are acknowledged in the New Testament, they are never central to the life of faith. Though undoubtedly more parabolic than historic, the image of communal sharing and economic interdependence, exemplified in Acts 2:44–45, challenges individualistic, work-driven approaches to life. The term *koinonia*, often translated as "fellowship," carries economic implications, emphasizing shared resources and mutual support over isolated labor. This vision of *koinonia* not only reorients economic relationships within the church but also serves as a critique of systems that prioritize individual productivity over communal well-being. It offers a countercultural model where mutual care supersedes economic self-sufficiency.

A Nuanced Theology of Work

In short, the biblical narrative resists simplistic affirmations of work as inherently good or necessary. From the harmonious tending of Genesis to the toil born of the fall, from Ecclesiastes's critique of labor's futility to the New Testament's radical re-prioritization of human values, Scripture challenges theologies that sanctify work without nuance. By subordinating work to the life of God's kingdom and emphasizing community, rest, and creativity, the biblical witness invites a reimagining of labor not as a burden to endure but as one dimension of a flourishing life under God's reign.

A THEOLOGY OF (NON) WORK: REIMAGINING LIFE BEYOND LABOR

As an alternative to the post-Reformation fusion of work and the Christian life—and reflecting the scriptural ambiguity surrounding labor—Jeremy Posadas offers a critical theological approach to nonwork. His perspective challenges the assumption that work is inherently good or necessary for human flourishing, critiquing the deep entanglement of labor with human identity and purpose. In his essay "The Refusal of Work in Christian Ethics and Theology," Posadas critiques traditional theological frameworks that valorize work and invites a reimagining of human life and community beyond the constraints of labor. His anti-work theology is a provocative but necessary corrective to dominant narratives that sanctify work.

Posadas begins by analyzing what he describes as the "common sense" of work in Christian theology, where labor is often portrayed as ontologically necessary and intrinsically good. This perspective, grounded in the analogy of "God the Worker," frames creation itself as divine labor and casts human work as a mirror of this creative act. Theologians like David Jensen have argued that human work fulfills the imago Dei, situating labor as an essential expression of humanity alongside rest, worship, and community. Even critiques of exploitative or alienating work tend to preserve this fundamental affirmation of labor's necessity, distinguishing between an idealized form of work and its corrupted manifestations under systems like capitalism. Efforts to redeem labor, such as advocating for economic democracy or fair wages, assume that the problem lies not in work itself but in the structures that distort it. Posadas, however, questions this underlying premise, suggesting that such theologies fail to account for the deeper domination that work exerts over human life.

Building on the insights of anti-work theorists such as Paul Lafargue, André Gorz, Kathi Weeks, Peter Frase, and Seth Ackerman, Posadas critiques the capitalist work ethic and explores alternative imaginaries that challenge the moral and cultural centrality of work in human life. A "work society," as Posadas critiques it, refers to a cultural framework in which productivity is seen as the highest measure of human value, marginalizing other dimensions of life such as rest, relationality, and creative expression. Under capitalism, work becomes a coercive necessity rather than a freely chosen activity. Most people must labor to survive, while a wealthy minority remain exempt. This dynamic transforms work into the primary mediator of access to basic needs, an arrangement Posadas argues is neither natural nor divinely ordained. He also critiques the cultural and moral framework of the "work ethic," which valorizes labor as virtuous and stigmatizes nonwork as laziness. This ethic sustains a "work society" where life revolves around productivity, reinforcing compliance with exploitative systems while marginalizing other modes of human flourishing.

The refusal of work, as Posadas envisions it, challenges the assumption that labor is central to human identity and dignity. Instead of laboring under the constraints of work, this perspective imagines a society where creativity, relationships, and rest take precedence. Posadas argues that human dignity should not be tied to productivity but recognized as an inherent gift from God. For instance, prioritizing relationships might involve creating rhythms of communal life that emphasize shared meals, collective care, and mutual support. Creativity could flourish in spaces where artistic and imaginative pursuits are not confined to leisure but seen as central to human flourishing. By decoupling dignity from labor, Posadas opens the door to alternative ways of living that prioritize joy and relationality over toil.

Theologically, Posadas critiques the tendency to equate divine action with human labor. Describing God's creative acts as "work" imposes human categories onto divine activity, raising questions about why these acts are labeled labor rather than play, art, or joy. This conflation reinforces the assumption that work is necessary and divinely sanctioned, even when theology seeks to "redeem" labor. For Posadas, efforts to improve work conditions or integrate individuals more fully into labor structures fail to challenge the fundamental dominance of work itself. Sabbath, often presented as a limitation on work's claims, still assumes work as the central organizing principle of life. However, this critique aligns with Jesus' teaching in Matt 11:28–30, where Jesus invites the weary and burdened to find rest in him—a rest that challenges the dominance of labor as the primary organizing principle of life. Posadas suggests that a more radical rethinking is required, one that subordinates work entirely.

In place of traditional frameworks, Posadas offers a vision of human flourishing that rejects labor's primacy. He imagines societal structures where basic needs—such as food, shelter, and healthcare—are guaranteed independently of work. This shift reframes human dignity as unconditional, rooted in God's provision rather than human productivity. Creativity and play, often sidelined in work-centric societies, are elevated as central to human identity. These activities, Posadas argues, reflect the divine joy of creation more authentically than labor under coercive systems. A theology of nonwork, therefore, celebrates rest, relationships, and imaginative living as primary expressions of human purpose.

Posadas's vision also carries practical implications for Christian ethics. Proposals like universal basic income and shorter workweeks are not merely economic reforms but theological imperatives that challenge Christians to advocate for systems that prioritize well-being over productivity. Vocation, too, must be reimagined. While figures like Dorothy Sayers have emphasized the intrinsic value of work as an expression of human creativity, Posadas invites a reevaluation of whether this emphasis unintentionally reinforces the dominance of labor over other aspects of life. No longer confined to economic roles, vocation can encompass caregiving, art, worship, and other activities that reflect God's relational and creative nature. In this way, Posadas's theology of nonwork invites Christians to embrace a broader understanding of human life, one that resists the dominance of labor and aligns more fully with the liberating message of the gospel.

By critiquing the theological valorization of work, Posadas opens space for alternative approaches that prioritize life over labor. His anti-work theology provides a crucial bridge to a theology of play, where joy, freedom, and communion with God take precedence over toil. As the next section will explore, a theology of play offers a compelling response to the dominance of work in theological anthropology, inviting Christians to imagine new ways of being that reflect the divine call to flourishing.

CONCLUSION

Work, as this chapter has demonstrated, is a deeply ambivalent aspect of human life. It can reflect divine creativity and offer a sense of purpose, but it can also become an oppressive force that alienates us from God, ourselves, and one another. Theologies of work from the Reformation to modern thinkers like Miroslav Volf highlight the sacred potential of labor while also grappling with the distortions introduced by sin and systemic inequities. At the same time, critical perspectives, such as Posadas's anti-work theology, challenge us to question whether work should occupy such a central place in our understanding of human flourishing.

This tension invites us to consider alternatives that transcend the work-centered narratives shaping both our culture and theology. What if our ultimate purpose is not defined by labor but by something more playful, relational, and liberating? Scripture itself hints at this possibility: from the joy of creation to Jesus' invitation to rest, from the Sabbath's rhythms to the *koinonia* of the early church. These threads point to a divine calling that celebrates not just work but also the rest, relationships, and creativity that reflect the fullness of God's design.

As we turn to the next chapter, we will explore a theology of play—a vision of life that prioritizes joy, freedom, and communion with God. Play, far from being trivial, serves as a profound theological metaphor and practice, inviting us to imagine and embody new ways of living that resist the dominance of labor and reflect the liberating hope of the gospel. Through play, we may glimpse the foretaste of the kingdom, where work and toil give way to delight, wonder, and flourishing in God's presence.

8

A Theology of Play

When I was in my mid-twenties, freshly out of college, I had a group of friends who would annually make a trip to the Oregon Coast for a seaside weekend away. Some of us had known each other since high school, others were new additions brought into the fold through romantic relationships or evolving friendships. We were all around the same age and shared a common thread: a background in evangelical church traditions, which many of us were in the process of reevaluating. These trips were a kind of sanctuary, a playful reprieve from the seriousness of postcollege life.

This was before Airbnb revolutionized travel, so the idea of pooling resources to rent a beach house still felt adventurous and novel. Jeff always took charge of finding the house, while Julian insisted on one close enough to the shore for us to spend the day on the beach. The Oregon Coast, even at the height of summer, often meant chilly winds and overcast skies. For many years, we huddled indoors reading books or perfecting cocktails (the biggest departure from our more conservative backgrounds!), but occasionally, the weather would cooperate, and we would spend hours building enormous, intricate sandcastles.

These were true group projects: some fetched buckets of icy Pacific water to pack the sand; others dug out moats and shaped towers; still others scavenged for shells, driftwood, or seaweed to decorate the walls and parapets. Julian, with his knack for artistry, created tiny fir trees by slowly dripping wet sand through his fingers, turning the castles into fantastical landscapes. To draw inspiration, we'd quote from *Monty Python and the*

Holy Grail or *The Lord of the Rings*, imagining that our constructions were part of these mythical worlds.

We chose our building spots strategically—far enough from the tide for workable sand but close enough for the finale we all eagerly anticipated: the rising tide's eventual destruction of our creation. Watching the waves slowly consume the castle became the highlight of the day, a reminder of life's impermanence and the sheer joy of shared creation. By the end, we were sunburned, exhausted, and full of laughter—spent not by obligation but by the kind of joyful effort that asks for nothing in return. There was no lingering sense of loss as the tide reclaimed our work, only the quiet satisfaction that comes from shared creation and the freedom to let go. In those hours of shaping sand, we stepped outside the demands of productivity, entering into something closer to play for its own sake.

I return to this memory because it bridges our previous conversation about the theologies of work with what I hope to present as an alternative framework for understanding human flourishing: a theology of play. In the last chapter, we critiqued the legacy of the Reformation's emphasis on work as grounded in God's ongoing activity in the world, and we explored Miroslav Volf's tripartite framework of work's protological, eschatological, and pneumatological significance. Yet, as I argued, this theological elevation of work risks overshadowing the biblical metaphor of Sabbath rest as both the original intent and eschatological goal of creation. Further, it struggles to speak to those subjected to dehumanizing or exploitative labor, as so powerfully articulated by Jeremy Posadas.

Americans spend most of our lives at work, and even when we're ostensibly at rest—watching TV or movies—our content often centers on work dynamics. Think of the early 2000s prevalence of workplace docucomedies like *The Office* or *Parks and Recreation*. Even in our downtime, we remain captivated by the rhythms of labor. But if work is neither what Scripture envisions as our origin (protology) nor our ultimate end (eschatology), what could serve as an alternative?

This chapter proposes play as such an alternative framework. Far from trivial, play can teach us both about the nature of God and God's desire for humanity. It embodies freedom, delight, and relational communion. Play reflects the unburdened joy of prelapsarian existence, where activity was free from toil. Its delight mirrors the goodness of creation as God declared it, allowing humanity to share in divine creativity. Its relational communion anticipates the eschatological banquet, where all creation gathers in celebration, free from alienation and brokenness.

In what follows, I will construct a theology of play that draws from philosophical insights, theological traditions, and practical applications for Christian ministry. Through this lens, play becomes not a distraction from life's purpose but a revelation of it—an invitation to encounter the God who delights in freedom, joy, and relationality.

A PHILOSOPHY OF PLAY

To construct a theology of play, it is essential to first explore play's philosophical roots, not as an intellectual exercise but as a pathway to reimagining human purpose and divine encounter. The works of Johan Huizinga and Hans-Georg Gadamer can give us the tools to recognize play as a sacred and revelatory mode of being, deeply aligned with the biblical rhythms of creation, rest, and worship.

Huizinga and Gadamer: Play as the Basis of Culture

In *Homo Ludens* (1938), Johan Huizinga argues that play is not a diversion from serious life but foundational to it. Cultures, rituals, and artistic expressions emerge from play's imaginative freedom. Central to his thought is the concept of the "magic circle"—a space set apart from ordinary routines where participants engage in voluntary, joyful acts governed by their own internal rules. This circle both creates freedom and establishes a boundary, suspending the ordinary rules of life. Within the magic circle, a new order governs, paralleling the sacred/secular divide in worship. Liturgy, like play, invites participants into a world where divine realities take precedence over the mundane.

For Huizinga, play carves out a space of freedom that resists the utilitarian work-focused logic that dominates modern life. Within this circle, participants step outside the demands of productivity, embracing the inherent worth of creativity and shared delight, like my friends and I working together to build a sandcastle on the beach. Theologically, this resonates with the Sabbath—a day hallowed by God not for its utility but for the sheer sacredness of joy (Gen 2:3). The Sabbath is not merely a cessation of labor but an invitation into divine play—a foretaste of the eschatological rest that Heb 4:9–11 frames as the destiny of God's people. Just as Sabbath disrupts the cycle of labor, play disrupts the narrative that life's value is measured by output. In play, as in worship, humanity encounters a glimpse of existence as it was meant to be: unburdened, relational, and infused with joy. Huizinga's understanding of play as a disruption of utilitarian logic reflects the sabbatical vision, where joy and relational presence stand at the center of creation's purpose.

Hans-Georg Gadamer extends this vision of play beyond cultural formation, situating it within the realm of being itself. In *Truth and Method*, Gadamer contends that play is not something we control but something that "plays" us. When we engage in play—whether in the arts, in conversation, or in worship—we surrender to its rhythm, allowing truth to emerge through participation. Gadamer highlights that play, like liturgy, unfolds organically. Just as dancers follow the rhythm without dictating the steps, worshipers engage in liturgy, allowing themselves to be carried by the movement of the Spirit. This interplay of freedom and form shapes both the participants and the community over time.

For Gadamer, the participatory nature of play closely parallels the act of worship. In liturgy, worshipers are not passive observers but active participants drawn into the divine drama. This participatory nature mirrors the dynamic movement of the Holy Spirit, drawing us into deeper communion with God. Liturgical play is akin to encountering a great work of art—one does not merely observe but is drawn into its movement, reshaped by the encounter. This resonates with the sacramental understanding of worship, where the Eucharist invites transformation through participation, not passive observation.

Gadamer's insight helps recover the mystery at the heart of Christian worship. Rather than reducing liturgy to mere work—something to be planned, executed, or completed—he invites us to see it as sacred play, a process in which God is not mastered but encountered through joyful surrender. In this light, the sanctuary becomes a kind of "magic circle" where heaven and earth meet and the church rediscovers its identity as the people of God.

BRIDGING PHILOSOPHY AND THEOLOGY

Huizinga and Gadamer offer a corrective to the modern idolization of labor, reclaiming play as a pathway to divine encounter. Huizinga's vision of culture as play draws attention to the ways human flourishing emerges through creativity and relational joy. Gadamer deepens this by suggesting that play may be a space where God's presence and truth break through, perhaps echoing Christ's words: "Unless you change and become like little children, you will never enter the kingdom of heaven" (Matt 18:3). Together, they challenge the church to resist the gravitational pull of productivity and rediscover the liberating power of play. In doing so, they help lay the groundwork for a theology of play—one that views the playful heart not as a distraction from the life of faith but as its very expression.

A THEOLOGY OF PLAY: PARTICIPATION IN DIVINE JOY AND LIBERATION

Building on the philosophical insights of Huizinga and Gadamer, mid-twentieth-century theologians began to explore play as a lens through which divine creativity, human flourishing, and eschatological hope could be understood. Thinkers like Hugo Rahner, Harvey Cox, and Jürgen Moltmann articulated a vision of play that resists reduction to frivolity. Instead, they present it as a participation in God's life, a prophetic critique of oppressive systems, and a foretaste of the kingdom of God.

Rahner: Play as Reflection of Divine Creativity

Hugo Rahner's *Man at Play* frames play as a sacred, foundational stance that humanity adopts before God—a mode of being that aligns with the rhythms of creation and mirrors divine joy. Rahner draws from Old Testament wisdom literature, Greek philosophy, and patristic thought to convey how play reflects the very nature of creation itself.

Central to Rahner's project is the conviction that creation is not a utilitarian act driven by necessity but a cosmic game—an expression of divine delight. In Prov 8, the figure of wisdom dances beside God as the world comes into being, offering a vision of creation as something beautiful, meaningful, and yet free from compulsion. Rahner sees in this image the sacred playfulness of God, suggesting that humanity's capacity for play echoes this divine joy. For Rahner, the incarnation and the church are the ultimate expressions of this divine play breaking into the world. Through Christ and the sacraments, humanity is drawn into the cosmic dance, liberated to participate in the ongoing creative joy of God. The church, in Rahner's view, becomes a playground of grace—a space where the seriousness of salvation history coexists with the lightness and wonder of divine life.

Rahner's theology stands in contrast to contemporary cultural distortions of play, where competition, commercialism, and entertainment overshadow freedom. In a world driven by productivity, Rahner's vision reminds us that genuine play emerges not from profit or escape but from the spiritual freedom to delight in God's presence. For Rahner, to play is to step into the divine game, where humanity is most fully alive.

Cox: Play as Prophetic Disruption

Harvey Cox's *The Feast of Fools* presents play as a prophetic and countercultural force—a necessary response to the sterility and rigidity of modern industrial society. Cox critiques Western Christianity for losing its capacity for celebration, fantasy, and festivity, suggesting that this loss mirrors the disenchantment of secular life. In Cox's theology, play becomes a form of resistance, challenging oppressive structures and reawakening the imagination of the church.

Cox introduces the concept of *homo festivus*—humanity as celebrant—alongside *homo fantasiae*, the imaginative critic. Together, these dimensions embody *homo religiosus*, the fullness of human engagement with God. Festivity invites communal joy and renewal, while fantasy subverts dominant narratives, allowing for new visions of the world to emerge. For Cox, the church's recovery of festivity is not merely aesthetic but theological. The Eucharist, understood as a *feast of fools*, disrupts the seriousness of empire and offers a vision of the kingdom where joy and abundance overflow. This festive imagination, Cox argues, must extend beyond liturgy, permeating the church's engagement with social justice, art, and community life.

While Cox's approach is speculative and sometimes provocative, his insistence that play can unmask the idolatries of modernity calls the church to rediscover the transformative power of joy. In his vision, the church becomes a site of holy subversion—where laughter, celebration, and creativity testify to the God who is making all things new.

A Theology of Play

Moltmann: Play as Eschatological Liberation

Jürgen Moltmann's *Theology of Play* situates play within the eschatological horizon, portraying it as a sign of the freedom and joy that characterize God's coming kingdom. For Moltmann, the structures of modern life—defined by work, achievement, and ethical striving—fail to account for the gratuity and grace of redeemed existence. Play, by contrast, offers a glimpse of the world made new, where humanity is liberated to delight in creation without fear or compulsion.

Moltmann frames divine acts—creation, incarnation, and redemption—as playful expressions of God's freedom. In contrast to the rigidity of modern leisure, which often mirrors the demands of labor, Moltmann envisions play as liberated space where the constraints of necessity are lifted. The church, he argues, becomes a "testing ground of the Kingdom," enacting the joy and spontaneity of the eschaton even now.[1] Yet, Moltmann's vision is not escapist. He acknowledges that play exists within the tension of the already and not yet. While play anticipates the joy of the resurrection, it also serves as a form of resistance—proclaiming life and hope in the face of suffering and death. In this way, play becomes a sign of protest, a refusal to submit to despair, and a foretaste of the redeemed creation. Moltmann warns, however, that play must remain grounded in grace. It cannot become an idol or an end in itself but must point beyond to the liberating joy of God. For Moltmann, the cross and resurrection stand as reminders that true playfulness is born from the freedom of redemption—a freedom that resists the powers of death and inaugurates the kingdom of life.

The Unifying Thread: Play as Participation

Though distinct in emphasis, Rahner, Cox, and Moltmann share a central conviction: play is not extraneous to the life of faith but essential to it. Whether reflecting the divine image, subverting oppressive systems, or anticipating eschatological joy, play draws humanity deeper into the life of God. Rahner's "play as reflection," Cox's "play as critique," and Moltmann's "play as liberation" converge to form a rich tapestry that challenges the church to reclaim play as a spiritual discipline. In embracing this vision, the church resists the gravitational pull of productivity and seriousness, rediscovering the grace, joy, and freedom at the heart of God's kingdom.

---

1. Moltmann et al., *Theology of Play*, 58.

Section 3: Theology at Work and Play

A TRIPARTITE THEOLOGY OF PLAY: PROTOLOGICAL, ESCHATOLOGICAL, AND PNEUMATOLOGICAL DIMENSIONS

The reflections of Rahner, Cox, and Moltmann highlight play as a thread running through creation, salvation, and the life of the church. Their insights suggest play to be far more than leisure or childlike diversion—it emerges as a mode of existence deeply attuned to the divine. From the cosmic dance of creation to the joy of the eschatological feast, play echoes the rhythms of God's engagement with the world. This theological depth invites a closer integration of play into Christian life and thought. By drawing on Miroslav Volf's tripartite framework of work (discussed in the previous chapter), we can articulate how play is woven into the fabric of divine and human experience—rooted in the beginning, reaching toward the eschaton, and animated by the Spirit in the present.

Protological Perspective: Play in the Beginning

Protology invites us to consider play as intrinsic to God's design for creation—woven into humanity's original vocation, long before toil and alienation entered the world. The opening chapters of Genesis depict humanity's first tasks as *tending* the garden (Gen 2:15) and *being fruitful and multiplying* (Gen 1:28). While these activities involve engagement with creation, they lack the burdens of frustration or survival that characterize postlapsarian labor. Instead, they reflect an effortless and joyous participation in divine creativity—marked more by play than by work as we typically understand it.

The image of humanity in Eden mirrors Johan Huizinga's description of play in *Homo Ludens*: voluntary, creative, and absorbing. Just as a child (or a group of twenty-somethings!) builds sandcastles for the sake of creation itself, so the tending of the garden can be seen as an expression of delight—purposeful yet unburdened by utility. In this sense, human vocation aligns with the rhythms of divine play, reflecting the freedom and joy embedded in God's creative act.

The command to "be fruitful and multiply" similarly reflects the generative, communal nature of play. Before the fall, this fruitfulness is a reflection of divine abundance. Hans-Georg Gadamer's notion of liturgy as play reinforces this vision—suggesting that prelapsarian activities like tending and fruitfulness might be understood as acts of worshipful play. In Eden, labor and celebration, work and leisure, are indistinguishable, revealing the original unity of creation in joy and relationality. By reclaiming this vision, we are invited to reconsider our understanding of human flourishing—not as defined by productivity but by communion, creativity, and the delight of existing in harmony with God and creation.

Eschatological Perspective: Play in the Redeemed Creation

If protology anchors play in the past, eschatology extends it into the future, envisioning play as central to the fulfillment of creation. The redeemed creation, as described in Scripture, is a place of liberated freedom, relational joy, and intrinsic meaning—a world no longer defined by striving or scarcity. This vision of the eschaton closely aligns with the essence of play, where actions are undertaken not for survival but for their own sake, reflecting the gratuity and abundance of divine life.

The Sabbath command (Exod 20:8–11) foreshadows this eschatological reality, offering rest and joy as anticipations of the world to come. The Sabbath is like Huizinga's magic circle—a space set apart from ordinary time, where participants are drawn into sacred rhythms of delight and relational flourishing. Within the Sabbath, work ceases and play begins—not as trivial distraction but as participation in the eternal dance of God's kingdom. Eschatological play thus reframes human striving—not as a linear march toward progress but as dynamic participation in God's infinite creativity.

Pneumatological Perspective: Play in the Spirit

A pneumatological lens reveals how play becomes a locus for the Spirit's transformative power in the present. Just as the Spirit animates and sanctifies work, it also infuses play with creativity, relationality, and joy—turning ordinary moments into sacred encounters. This perspective invites us to see play as a Spirit-led practice that opens pathways to divine encounter and communal flourishing.

In worship, play emerges through liturgy and the arts, creating spaces where the Spirit fosters spontaneity and relational engagement. Gadamer's notion of play as a dynamic, truth-revealing process aligns with the Spirit's role in drawing worshipers into deeper communion with God. The unpredictability and freedom of play reflect the movement of the Spirit, who "blows where it wills" (John 3:8). In these moments of play, the Spirit transforms rigid forms of worship into vibrant, relational encounters with the divine.

Beyond worship, the Spirit infuses discipleship and community life with playful freedom. Practices like Godly Play, storytelling, and communal feasting cultivate wonder and openness, nurturing the fruits of the Spirit—love, joy, and peace—within the body of Christ. Through play, the Spirit forms Christlike character, deepens relationships, and invites the church to embody the joy of the kingdom now. In this sense, play becomes a spiritual discipline—one that resists the pressures of performance and productivity by inviting participants to dwell in God's presence with the lightness of a child at play.

A Holistic Theology of Play

By applying Volf's tripartite framework to play, we uncover its theological significance across protological, eschatological, and pneumatological dimensions. Play reflects humanity's original vocation in the harmonious rhythm of creation, anticipates the joy of the redeemed world, and serves as a Spirit-infused practice in the present. This holistic vision dissolves the false dichotomy between work and play, inviting us to see both as expressions of divine creativity and relational flourishing. Through this lens, play emerges as an essential means of encountering God in everyday life, calling the church to live into the freedom, joy, and relationality of God's kingdom—a summons to dance in the eternal rhythm of divine love.

FROM THEOLOGY TO PRACTICE: EMBODYING PLAY IN THE LIFE OF FAITH

The tripartite theology of play—rooted in creation, anticipating the eschaton, and animated by the Spirit—invites tangible expression in the rhythms of Christian life. If play is woven into the fabric of divine action and human vocation, then the church must learn not only to articulate this reality but to embody it. This embodiment raises pressing questions: How can worship, discipleship, and community life reflect the joyful, liberative play described by Rahner, Cox, and Moltmann? In what ways can the practices of the church disrupt the world's obsession with work and control, cultivating spaces where divine delight and relational freedom flourish?

A Theology of Play

The shift from theological reflection to practice is not a departure but a continuation—a recognition that the play of God finds its home not just in doctrine but in the lived everyday experience of the people of God. This next section explores how the church might recover play as a spiritual discipline, a form of liturgical imagination, and a foundation for building communities marked by joy, creativity, and grace.

Play as Spiritual Formation: From Children to the Whole Church

Theological reflection on play has long centered on children's spirituality, recognizing play as a natural and vital way for children to engage with the divine. Yet, this focus, while fruitful, risks confining play to a developmental stage rather than embracing it as a core practice for all people across the lifespan. By expanding the vision of play beyond childhood, the church can reclaim its transformative potential in worship, discipleship, and community life.

Play and Children's Spirituality: A Foundation for Encounter

Since the 1970s, psychologists and theologians—Maria Montessori, Erik Erikson, Jean Piaget, Lawrence Kohlberg, Ana-Maria Rizzuto, and James Fowler—have explored the intersections between developmental theory and spiritual growth. These insights have informed practices like Sofia Cavalletti's Catechesis of the Good Shepherd and Jerome Berryman's Godly Play, which view play not as distraction but as a sacred medium through which children encounter God.[2]

Berryman's Godly Play, for example, honors children's capacity for theological reflection by inviting them into tactile, participatory experiences with Scripture. In this space, biblical narratives are not simply taught but discovered, fostering awe, curiosity, and personal connection. Play, in this framework, becomes an act of wonder—a reminder that spirituality often emerges not through rigid instruction but through open-ended exploration.[3]

---

2. Cavalletti, *Religious Potential of the Child*; Berryman, *Godly Play*.
3. See also G. Green, *Imagining God*; Winnicott, *Playing and Reality*.

Section 3: Theology at Work and Play

Beyond Childhood: Play as a Lifelong Spiritual Discipline

While much of this work on play and spirituality centers on children, the spiritual significance of play is not confined to the early years. The same qualities that make play vital for children—imagination, relationality, and embodied learning—are equally transformative for adults and entire communities. If play reflects the freedom and delight of divine life, then it must hold significance across all stages of faith.

Jack Williams, in his article "Playing Church: Understanding Ritual and Religious Experience Resourced by Gadamer's Concept of Play," draws from Hans-Georg Gadamer to extend play into the whole life of the church. For Williams, play is not a preliminary step to "serious" faith but an ongoing mode of spiritual engagement that invites congregants into deeper rhythms of truth and encounter. Williams highlights forms of *God-play*—imaginative, sometimes whimsical practices that create space for intimate connection with God. Examples like setting a place for Jesus at the dinner table or engaging Scripture through artistic expression (like *fabricandi divina*, discussed earlier in this book) reflect the ways adults, too, can approach God through playful and participatory acts.

However, Williams raises an important caution: play must be balanced with theological integrity. While God-play can nurture intimacy with the divine, it risks trivialization if detached from the core truths of the faith. This tension invites discernment—how can the church cultivate playful engagement while ensuring that it remains rooted in sound doctrine and reverence?

The Sanctuary as Playground: Embodying Play in Worship

J. Patrick Vaughn furthers this conversation by proposing the church as a metaphorical playground, drawing on Donald Winnicott's concept of the "holding environment." In his article "The Sanctuary as Playground," Vaughn imagines worship spaces as areas of both safety and creative risk—a bounded yet liberative environment where congregants encounter God and one another. This metaphor challenges the assumption that worship must always be solemn, opening the door for liturgical practices that embrace joy, experimentation, and communal participation.

Vaughn describes how the sanctuary, like a playground, invites participants into exploration and relational vulnerability. In his vision, confirmation classes, participatory storytelling, and artistic rituals all reflect this playful dynamic, fostering spiritual maturity through embodied practice. Vaughn's approach echoes Fowler's emphasis on experiential learning, suggesting that faith deepens when people actively engage—emotionally and physically—with the sacred.

Reimagining Play Across Generations

By embracing play as a lifelong practice, the church can rediscover its identity as a community shaped by joy and relational freedom. Garrett Green's description of imagination as the faculty by which we pattern experiences and meaning underscores the essential role of play in shaping how Christians engage Scripture, theology, and the world.[4] Moreover, communal acts of play—feasts, storytelling, artistic endeavors—reflect the eschatological vision of play described by Cox and Moltmann. In these moments, the church rehearses the joy of the kingdom, where human striving gives way to celebration and grace.

Ultimately, the call to play is not merely for children but for all God's people. In embracing play, the church reclaims its vocation to reflect the image of a God who delights in creation, a Christ who welcomed the little children, and a Spirit who dances through the life of the faithful.

CONCLUSION: THE SACRED CALL TO PLAY

A theology of play invites us to reimagine human existence and divine engagement through the interconnected lenses of creativity, joy, and relationality. Far from being a frivolous or secondary pursuit, play emerges as a key theological concern—woven into the fabric of creation and redemptive history. At its core, play reflects the freedom and delight of God's creative act, revealing that humanity's first calling was not to labor under compulsion but to joyfully tend the world as co-creators with God. This freedom echoes the relational communion of the Trinity, where love and generosity flow in eternal interplay, inviting us to step into the divine dance. In this light, play is a mirror of divine life—a reminder that the God who crafted the universe did so with joy and delight. Moreover, play holds within it an eschatological hope, offering glimpses of the world as it will be when all things are made

---

4. G. Green, *Imagining God*, 151.

Section 3: Theology at Work and Play

new. It serves as a foretaste of the great banquet, where joy, freedom, and relational flourishing will mark the fullness of God's kingdom.

Section 4
Everyday Theology in Institutional Life

FROM PLAY TO INSTITUTIONAL LIFE

As we transition from exploring the theology of play to a more structured focus on administration and leadership within institutional life, it might seem like a jarring shift. After all, play evokes creativity, freedom, and spontaneity, while administration often conjures images of meetings, budgets, and strategic plans. Yet, this transition reflects a profound truth—so much of our lives are lived within institutions. Whether through our work, educational endeavors, or engagement with the church, we encounter God not just in moments of joy or contemplation but in the complexities of shared institutional life.

The chapters that follow, centered on academic administration and institutional discernment, continue the exploration of theology's presence in everyday experience. They argue that the spaces where decisions are made, policies crafted, and missions discerned are not devoid of divine activity. Rather, they are fertile grounds for theological reflection and practice.

In particular, chapter 9 introduces the concept of theological administration, likening the role of academic deans to that of deacons within the church. This metaphor, drawn from the renewed diaconate, reimagines administrative leadership as a form of service that embodies message bearing, agency, and attentive stewardship. Just as deacons stand at the threshold between the altar and the congregation, so too do deans occupy a liminal

Section 4: Everyday Theology in Institutional Life

space between faculty and institutional leadership, facilitating communication and shepherding the community.

Chapter 10 extends this focus by reflecting on the institutional life of General Theological Seminary, particularly the process of navigating change through a theological lens. Faced with existential challenges, the seminary's leadership turned to Anglican frameworks of reason, tradition, and Scripture to guide their decisions. This discernment process, grounded in the Paschal mystery, illustrates how theology can shape and sustain even the most complex institutional transitions.

Both chapters illuminate the broader conviction that theology is not confined to church pews or academic texts but permeates the boardrooms, faculty lounges, and administrative offices where institutional life unfolds. By inviting readers into the theological reflections of academic leaders, this section affirms that working with others—resolving conflicts, navigating crises, or envisioning futures—can become acts of faith and opportunities for encountering God.

This shift from play to administration may feel abrupt, but it reflects the rhythms of life itself—where moments of joyful creativity are often interwoven with seasons of careful stewardship and structured leadership. In this way, the work of leading institutions becomes not just a professional task but a form of faithful engagement with the world.

9

A Theology of Administration

INTRODUCTION

RATHER THAN SEEING ALL work as abstractly aligned with God's purposes for the world, what if our faith shaped how we specifically understand work? This is to say, is there something about the Christian life and way that might uniquely change how we interpret or engage in our professional lives?

A call to academic administration is, for some of us, a difficult thing to first explain or defend to our colleagues in the ranks of the professoriate. Though as scholars we still retain a passion for classroom teaching, academic research, and exploring the deep ideas of our disciplines, those of us who have journeyed to the "dark side" of academic administration also feel a deep sense of vocational fulfillment when we work through complex organizational problems, curricular design matters, quality assurance, assessment and accreditation issues, and other strategic and systematic institutional concerns. When we talk about such work with our colleagues, it is not infrequent for them to respond with a mix of bafflement (that someone actually enjoys such tasks) and relief (that they don't have to do them!).

For some time now, I've been looking for a way to theologically frame my work as an academic dean so that I could both explain this career choice to my theological colleagues and offer to other new deans a way of thinking theologically about our call to, and identity within, academic administration.[1] In the process of researching this idea, I stumbled upon insights

---

1. At the time I wrote this, I worked at a Lutheran seminary, and it was tempting to

that have emerged from recent ecumenical discussions of the permanent and distinctive diaconate that seem to me to offer a helpful framework for thinking about the dean's particular vocation. In this chapter I want to play with a metaphorical affinity between the "renewed diaconate"[2] and a vocation in academic administration. Using John Collins's work on the diaconate as a guide, I will argue that his threefold description of how a deacon serves both within and on behalf of the church (as message bearer, responsible agent, and attendant) can provide a useful framework for thinking theologically about what I suggest calling "deaconly deans" of theological schools.

A BIT ABOUT DEACONS[3]

Though the early church might likely have had a very rich understanding of the office of the deacon, a distinctive diaconate fades into relative obsolescence after about the fourth century. Barnett argues that in the post-Constantinian church, the diaconate evolved into a *cursus honorum* and was subsumed into the episcopate as the first stage of the threefold order of deacon, priest, and bishop.[4] After this, in the medieval Western Church, the distinctive role of the deacon seems primarily to appear only in high liturgies, where the part of deacon would be played by priests who, wearing the dalmatic, served as deacon only in dress.[5] Given the limited ministerial or theological significance of the diaconate in the medieval Western Church, it is not surprising that by the sixteenth century, many of the Continental

---

think about this call either through the lens of the Lutheran theology of "vocation" (for Lutherans, all work which God calls us to, whether to the parish, the field, or the factory, is part of our calling by God to service in his world) or perhaps by grouping the work of an administrator into God's "left-hand kingdom." Though both of these concepts offer some promising sources of reflection, neither seemed to give due theological dignity to the role of the administrator, nor did they allow me to properly situate the academic administrator within Paul's listing of gifts in 1 Cor 12:27–28.

2. Elsewhere, renewed diaconate may be called the "distinctive diaconate" or the "permanent diaconate" in contrast with the "transitional diaconate."

3. Among these, John Collins, *Diakonia* and *Diakonia Studies*; and Barnett, *Diaconate* are of particular note. See also Anthony Thiselton's reception of Collins and Barnett in *First Epistle to the Corinthians*, 300. Also, the Lutheran World Federation report, though less concerned with the implications of Collins and Barnett, does indicate a shift toward the new diaconate and away from the "loving service" model that has historically been the approach taken by world Lutheranism (Nordstokke, "*Diakonia* in Context").

4. Barnett, *Diaconate*, 103.

5. John Collins, *Diakonia*, 3.

Reformers sought to do away with the office entirely[6] or, as in the case with Luther, sought to absorb the diaconate into broader laicized ministries that were without expressly liturgical function.[7]

The next major transition in the diaconate happened in the mid-nineteenth century, first among German Lutherans, then quickly followed by Anglicans, Methodists, and Roman Catholics. In 1836, Pastor Theodor Fliedner founded the Deaconesses of Kaiserswert. This female-only order was committed to providing education, nursing, and service to the poor and homeless. Similar orders cropped up within the churches of the Anglican Communion, notably in the Church of England in the form of the Mildmay Deaconesses (1860), in the Episcopal Church through the American Deaconess Society (1872), and eventually in the Church of South India, which instituted an ordained, permanent diaconate in 1947. Within the Roman Catholic Church, the development of a distinctive diaconate was deeply influenced by Karl Rahner's work leading up to the Second Vatican Council.

Admittedly, it is unfair to treat all of these developments in the diaconate as one thing. Between these churches, there were differences in who was eligible to join the order or office (male or female), whether the diaconate was dedicated exclusively to welfare or education, and whether such a calling involved ordination or commissioning. Despite these nuances, a common theme uniting nearly all post-mid-nineteenth-century diaconal movements was the central understanding of diaconal ministry as "loving service,"[8] which is based upon what Anthony Gooley refers to as "deacons and the servant myth."[9] This trend has its roots in a particular interpretation of *diakonos* that skews service in a direction of menial servitude. Brodd, following Collins, suggests that this trend was in part the result of a conflation of *caritas* and *diaconia* that limited how diaconal ministry was construed by the churched to works of charity.[10] The interpretation of *diakonos* supported by Brodd, Collins, Barnet, etc., paints with a much broader palette the activities that could typify diaconal service.

Collins's work is of particular note. In his *Diakonia: Reinterpreting the Ancient Sources*, he presents a study of the wide use of *diakon-* words in literature from the period of the New Testament. In his research, he

6. John Collins, *Diakonia*, 2.
7. Barnett, *Diaconate*, 157.
8. Barnett, *Diaconate*, 157.
9. Gooley, "Deacons and Servant Myth."
10. Brodd, "*Caritas* and *Diakonia*."

found no evidence that *diakonia* was ever associated with menial service or special humility. His work suggests that when the church began calling deacons, the choice of this word would have likely conveyed images more associated with ambassadors, envoys, or messengers than strictly stewards, servants, or workers of charity. To this end, deacons would have likely played an important strategic role in leading and stewarding the mission of early Christian communities,[11] particularly through their close relationship between deacons and the oversight of the bishop. Indeed, much of the deacon's work could be construed as working through the agency of the bishop for the benefit of their communities. As such, the diaconal ministry was both deeply relational and collaborative.[12]

In their attempt to appropriate Collins's research into their own construal of the diaconate, a working party of the General Assembly of the Church of England has suggested that the ministries of those called to the permanent diaconate could be framed by the following three traits:

- Message Bearing—A deacon is a spokesperson, an envoy, a courier, or a go-between, who is entrusted with important tidings.
- Agent—A deacon is an ambassador, a mediator, a person who is given a commission to carry out a task and to act on behalf of someone in authority.
- Attendant—A deacon is one who is entrusted with the oversight of the affairs of a person or a household, not one who simply serves or waits table.[13]

DEACONS AND DEANS

Looking at the list above, parallels between the work of a deacon and the work of an academic dean become easy to make. As a messenger, the dean plays a vital role in translating the needs and concerns of the faculty to the administration and translating the needs and concerns of the administration to the faculty. As a responsible agent who acts on behalf of the president-board, the dean serves their communities relationally through collaborative leadership. Finally, as an attendant, the dean plays a vital role

---

11. John Collins, *Diakonia*, 227–44.
12. John Collins, *Diakonia*, 128.
13. Archbishop's Council, *For Such a Time*.

in stewarding the vision and mission of their school through the faithful management of everyday affairs.

Deans and deacons both find themselves situated within the midst of complex organizations—deacons between bishops and their churches, and deans between their president-boards and their faculties. In this location, both deans and deacons exercise leadership "from the middle." I want to use the metaphor of a deaconly dean to think about how deans of theological schools can not only lead from the middle but thrive in the middle.

DEANS AS MESSENGERS

As identified by Collins's work, those who served in *diakon-* roles frequently were tasked with ferrying information between competing parties. This particular task of being a middle point in a complex communication system is one of the more privileged roles played by deaconly deans. Deaconly deans stand in the middle of the often-competing worlds of the faculty and the administration. Communication to both groups requires the dean to become proficient in two different kinds of language. An academic dean must be able to understand the broader matters of finance or assessment and have the competence to provide creative input into the strategic management and leadership of the institution as a whole. This may involve writing in the language of annual reports, strategic plans, or self-studies, and speaking in the language of board dinners, cabinet meetings, or executive summaries. Yet the dean must also be able to thrive and excel in the world of scholarship, convey a deep commitment to student learning, and stand shoulder to shoulder with the faculty of his or her institution. Being fluent in both languages, and feeling at home in either culture, allows the deaconly dean to translate the needs and concerns of either group to the other.

Though their service as a messenger requires deaconly deans to be gifted communicators, more important yet is the gift of being a deep listener. Deaconly deans, standing in the middle of their schools, are able to hear and collect the dreams and missional aspirations of their schools, as expressed by the administration, the faculty, and the students. Through deep, attentive listening, the dean gathers and curates the school's living and spoken vision and then speaks back this vision to the community as a whole. A deaconly dean succeeds at being a messenger when their work serves to bring about not only honest communication between the various facets of the institution but a common vision of the institution's shared mission.

DEANS AS AGENTS

Responsible agency is the delegation of authority to act from one party to another. A possible biblical example of a deacon who serves as a responsible agent might be Phoebe, who is mentioned at the conclusion of Paul's Letter to the Romans. Paul commends to the church of Rome "our sister Phoebe, a deacon of the church at Cenchraea, so that you may welcome her in the Lord as is fitting for the saints, and help her in whatever she may require from you, for she has been a benefactor of many and myself as well" (Rom 16:1–2). Phoebe is sent to Rome as Paul's delegate, and Paul seems to expect the Roman church to receive this deaconess as if they were receiving himself. It is in this vein that the renewed diaconate paradigm frames the authority of the deacon as authority that is delegated to the deacon by the bishop.

In our present discussion, one could argue that for deaconly deans, the authority to lead and the responsibility to manage are delegated to them by their president-boards. In theological schools, the relationship between dean and president is a particularly close one. As McClean notes in *Leading from the Center*, the office of the dean in freestanding seminaries didn't become commonplace until the 1950s. Until this time, presidents were expected to serve as both the chief executive officer and the chief academic officer of their institutions. However, as the role of presidents evolved and the external (largely fundraising) duties of the president increased, stand-alone deans emerged from the office of the president to provide daily management and leadership within the institution.[14]

I once worked under a president who described leadership as the application of power toward a creative and constructive purpose. Deaconly deans who aspire to lead in ways that are genuinely creative and constructive must remain conscious of the source of their delegated authority and carry it with humility, recognizing that it is entrusted to them by another. Such deans do not wield authoritarian power to control their institutions, nor do they impose their personal vision or mission upon them. Rather, deans are called to serve on behalf of their presidents, for the benefit of their communities, and through the trust they have earned from their faculty.

---

14. McLean, *Leading from the Center*, 17–18.

DEANS AS ATTENDANTS

Though Collins reminds his readers that the "attendance" of the deacon would have meant oversight of household affairs and not just table waiting, it is worth reflecting here on the inherited liturgical role played by deacons as eucharistic attendants. Marking the deacon from the presiding priest is the distinctive way that the deacon's stole is worn—almost like a sash—over the left shoulder alone. The reason for this is both practical and symbolic. Practically, it prevents the stole from interfering with the deacon's work of setting the eucharistic table and assisting the president in his or her duties. Symbolically, it reminds the congregation that the deacon is prepared to jump into action at a moment's notice should some urgent issue arise. Deacons may not preside at the Eucharist, but as "liturgical managers" they ensure that the table is prepared, the prayers are introduced, and the liturgical actions are rightly explained. In so doing, deacons ensure that priest and congregation are able to participate fully in worship.

I find attendance to be a powerful metaphor for exploring what makes up the day-to-day service of a deaconly dean. A dean's day can be filled with any variety of activities, ranging from evaluating transfer credits from students' transcripts, to addressing plagiarism violations, to planning faculty development activities, to preparing for accreditation visits. Though the quotidian life of a dean may not seem glamorous, deans have been charged by our presidents and our communities with attending to the faithful management of our schools. Such management amounts to being a "good steward" of the mission of the school. The dean occupies a unique position within the school, one that allows them to provide the necessary infrastructure to support and drive positive changes. Effective stewardship challenges the dean to leverage the resources at their disposal to enable and sustain the school's mission.

Management is clearly one of the least "sexy" aspects of leadership. It is far less about steering and the framing vision of the school than it is about tending to the smooth and efficient operation of the system. Yet without effective management, the very vision that leadership casts would be unsuccessful and without implementation. Like deacons who aid the priest and the congregation to participate in worship, deaconly deans help the administration and faculty to enter fully into the mission of their schools.

In conclusion, I want to offer just one more picture of the leadership of deaconly deans by turning to another scriptural metaphor. Paul's list of spiritual gifts in 1 Cor 12:28 offers a tantalizing glimpse into the sorts of activities and roles that might have been indicative of the first-century church. Paul writes, "God has placed in the church *first of* all apostles, *second* prophets, *third* teachers, *after that* miracles, *then* the gifts of healings, helping, leadership, varieties of tongues." Biblical scholars, of course, debate about the significance of this ordering (Does this imply the prioritization of one gift/role/office over another? Does this reflect an early hierarchy? Does this list have liturgical significance?). What I find interesting about this one verse is a single word, which in the whole of the New Testament occurs only here. This *hapax legomenon* is the Greek word *kubernesis*, which in English has been rendered as "leadership," "guidance," and "administration" in various translations. *Kubernao* (and its related word in Latin *gubernare*) figuratively means to steer or pilot a boat as a helmsman.

I find it interesting that Paul uses a word that is borrowed from the maritime trade to name a particular activity that goes on in the church. I suppose it's not all that different from our current practice, in church leadership circles, of borrowing phrases taken from business and the economy (such as marketing, promotion, executive leadership) to describe the tasks associated with leading churches. Yet the metaphors or images that are connoted by a helmsman, on the one hand, and a captain or chief executive, on the other, are positionally different. The captain or chief executive flies the plane from the front and leads the institution at the top, whereas the helmsman—with hand on the tiller—steers, directs, and leads the ship from the rear.

Helmsmen are able to stay on course and can quickly adapt and respond to changes in weather and wave. Yet a helmsman's gaze isn't set on the distant port alone; their vision passes through from stern to crew, through sails to bow, all on its way to the horizon beyond. They are leaders *and* managers, adept at responding to what we might call both adaptive and technical challenges. Yet it is only by being located in the back of the boat that the helmsman is given space to develop a vision that encompasses the whole ecology of the ship, inclusive of ship, crew, and the direction in which the ship is headed.

It makes sense, if leading is in some ways about steering from the back, that *kubernesis* is listed at the penultimate spot in Paul's list. For our purposes, it seems that this style of leadership has a lot in common with what I've described as deaconly deans (who communicate as message bearers, lead through responsible agency, and manage as attendants). Leaders in the writings of Paul and deaconly deans may not find themselves surrounded by the pomp and honor that come with other more public roles (chief executives, presidents, captains), but in a kingdom where the last are first and the first are last, deans should embrace steering from the back of the boat.

10

A Theology of Leadership in Theological Education

INTRODUCTION

HIGHER EDUCATION IN THE United States is undergoing a generational transformation driven by economic, demographic, and societal changes that threaten the viability of many institutions. While closures and retrenchments dominate headlines, theological schools have often pursued partnerships or affiliations as an alternative to closure, preserving their mission through innovative approaches. This chapter explores how General Theological Seminary navigated such a transformation through a discernment process shaped by theological commitments.

At first glance, institutional leadership in theological education may seem far removed from the themes of creativity, play, and work explored in this book. However, the story of General Seminary illustrates another dimension of how theology informs and shapes everyday life—including organizational decisions. By embracing the Anglican framework of reason, tradition, and Scripture, General's leadership discerned a path that honored its historic mission while embracing a new future. This narrative reflects the lived theology of everyday life in the context of institutional change.

A Theology of Leadership in Theological Education

THE LANDSCAPE OF THEOLOGICAL EDUCATION

The challenges facing theological schools mirror broader trends in higher education: declining enrollment, financial pressures, and shifting cultural perceptions of education's value. For theological institutions, these challenges are compounded by changing religious landscapes, particularly for mainline denominations.

ABOUT GENERAL SEMINARY

The General Theological Seminary is the oldest continuously operating stand-alone Anglican seminary in the world. It was founded in 1817 to train clergy in the Protestant Episcopal Church, the successor body to the Church of England in America following the US War of Independence. For most of its history, the seminary has been located on a city block in New York's Chelsea neighborhood, on land gifted by Clement Clarke Moore, famed author of the Christmas poem "A Visit from St. Nicholas." Within decades of its establishment, the seminary faced mounting financial costs, deteriorating infrastructure, and competition from newly founded Episcopal seminaries across the growing country. By the 1860s, a near closure was narrowly avoided through a combination of aggressive fundraising and the late nineteenth-century economic boom that revitalized New York City.

Under the leadership of Dean Eugene Augustus Hoffman, who served from 1879 to 1902, the seminary underwent significant transformation. Hoffman sought to restore General Seminary to its position as the flagship training institution for the Episcopal Church. He envisioned a grand campus modeled after Oxford's quadrangles, incorporating study spaces, improved housing, a world-class library, and the magnificent neo-Gothic Chapel of the Good Shepherd, consecrated in 1888. This ambitious vision was realized largely through Hoffman's connections with New York's elite, whose generosity ensured the seminary's growth.[1]

Despite its storied history, the seminary faced challenges in the twentieth and twenty-first centuries as the Episcopal Church and its supporting structures underwent significant decline. The shifting cultural and financial landscapes necessitated innovative approaches to sustain its mission, leading to the strategic decisions and discernment processes explored in this chapter.

---

1. Dawley, *General Theological Seminary*.

Section 4: Everyday Theology in Institutional Life

RECENT HISTORY

I arrived at General in 2016 to take a call as the seminary's academic dean and vice president for academic affairs. In the decade preceding my arrival, the seminary had weathered two difficult controversies. The first, in 2007, was an unsuccessful attempt to construct a revenue-generating high-rise tower and hotel conference center. This ambitious project had had the potential to create an almost entirely self-sustaining financial model for the seminary. However, the failure to complete the tower plunged the institution into financial peril, culminating in the sale of nearly $100 million of seminary property in 2010 to clear debts, repay its own endowments, and address urgent deferred maintenance needs.[2]

The second difficulty occurred in 2014, with a highly publicized and painful conflict between the seminary's administration and its faculty. This dispute resulted in the dismissal of nearly the entire faculty and the de facto elimination of tenure.[3] These two crises, combined with a prolonged period of enrollment decline in the seminary's core program—the full-time, residential, ordination-track master of divinity degree—created significant challenges for the institution. At its height in 2007, the MDiv program enrolled ninety-seven students, making it one of the largest in the Episcopal Church. By 2021, total enrollment in the program had dropped to fewer than ten, with only two new first-year matriculants that year. Recognizing the urgency of the situation, the board and administration launched a comprehensive evaluation of the seminary's operational and programmatic models.

During late winter 2021, I led a research project funded by the Lilly Endowment's "Pathways for Tomorrow: Phase 1" grant. This project, titled "Partners in Formation," included an alumni survey, structured conversations with regional stakeholders about the future of theological education, and an analysis of nearly a decade's worth of internal data compared with data from other Anglican/Episcopal and mainline theological schools. Through this work, we gained a clearer understanding of the seminary's enrollment decline and operational fragility.

Our findings revealed that General's enrollment losses far exceeded those of peer institutions, indicating a waning market share of ordination-track students. The high cost of operating a stand-alone seminary in New York City also meant that the institution spent more per student than 95

---

2. ENS Staff, "General Seminary Strikes Pact."
3. Otterman, "Seeking Dean's Firing."

percent of other ATS-accredited schools. These insights prompted the board to confront significant adaptive challenges, such as reimagining the financial model, leveraging campus resources more effectively, and addressing the accessibility and affordability of theological education.

We realized that traditional strategies—enrollment management, capital campaigns, property development, or new charismatic leadership—would not suffice. Instead, we needed to embrace adaptive leadership, which Ronald Heifetz defines as requiring changes in values, beliefs, or behaviors and engaging in deep learning and innovation.[4] This framework guided our efforts to envision a future for General Seminary that honored its mission while responding to new realities.

A METHODOLOGY FOR DISCERNMENT: REASON, TRADITION, AND SCRIPTURE

The magnitude of our challenge necessitated a complete rethinking of how the seminary operated. In June of 2021, our board launched an initiative that we called "Strategic and Faithful Partnerships," which had three goals: arrive at a clear sense of the challenge at hand; foster a community of discernment among the board; empower the board to make difficult—but faithful and strategic—action in support of the mission.

In order for the Strategic and Faithful Partnerships initiative to be successful, the board would need to cultivate the capacity to navigate three sometimes-competing sources of information: a data-informed understanding of our present reality; a tradition-informed understanding of institutional mission; and a theologically informed sense of our place within the broader story of God's transformative work in the world.

Fortunately, as a seminary of the Episcopal Church, this threefold approach closely resembled another well-beloved threefold framework commonly known as the "three-legged stool." This methodological metaphor, rooted in Anglican theology, represents the three sources of authority that shape Anglican belief and practice: reason, tradition, and Scripture.

The concept finds its origins in the writings of Richard Hooker, the great defender of the Elizabethan settlement. In his opus, *Laws of Ecclesiastical Polity*, Hooker argued that reason, tradition, and Scripture were all necessary for arriving at a proper understanding of Christian faith and practice:

---

4. Heifetz, *Leadership Without Easy Answers*, 22.

SECTION 4: EVERYDAY THEOLOGY IN INSTITUTIONAL LIFE

> What Scripture doth plainly deliver, to that the first place both of credit and obedience is due; the next whereunto is whatsoever any man can necessarily conclude by force of reason; after the third the consent of antiquity.[5]

This tripartite methodology underscores the equal importance of these three sources of authority as one arrives at a comprehensive understanding of Christian faith. Twentieth-century Anglican theologian Bishop Stephen Sykes humorously quipped, "The Church of England has always claimed that its life and practice are based on three 'legs' of authority: the Bible, tradition, and reason. It has been said that if one of these legs is missing, the stool falls over."[6] In practice, the so-called three-legged stool guides theological reflection and decision-making within Anglicanism, serving as "a way of holding together the diverse elements within the Anglican tradition."[7]

Although the board was not being asked to debate the fine points of Anglican ecclesiology (which is how Hooker used his own methodology in the seventeenth century), we were being asked to achieve a nuanced understanding of the mission and future of our institution. As a guide to this work, we adopted Hooker's threefold method to shape our discernment process.

In the place of "reason" in Hooker's methodology, we sought to engage in data-informed analysis and assessment, what I called "dwelling in the data." In the place of "tradition" in Hooker's methodology, we sought to gain a clearer sense of the seminary's historic mission, ethos, and legacy, a process we called "learning our story." Last, in the place of "Scripture" in Hooker's methodology, we sought to develop a shared story, grounded in the Paschal mystery, which emboldened us to believe in the transformative power of God at work in our institution.

Reason: Dwelling in the Data

> The light therefore, which is the star of natural reason and wisdom casteth, is too bright to be obscured by the mist of a word or two uttered to diminish that opinion . . . even in matters that touch most nearly the principal duties of men and the glory of the eternal God.[8]

5. Hooker, *Laws of Ecclesiastical Polity*, 2:207.
6. Sykes, *Study of Anglicanism*, 1.
7. Chapman, *Anglicanism*, 32.
8. Hooker, *Laws of Ecclesiastical Polity*, 1:3.7.17.

Hooker describes reason as a divinely given human faculty that encompasses the ability to draw logical deductions, analyze evidence, and make rational judgments. Hooker emphasized the significance of reason in safeguarding Christian theology from succumbing to scriptural literalism or traditionalism, which he associated—respectively—with the views of the radically Reformed Puritans or Roman Catholics in his time.

At General Seminary, we embraced reason as an integral part of our discernment process, characterized by an open-eyed and data-informed approach to decision-making. We sought to evaluate our prayerful hopes for the seminary's future and our faithful remembrance of its historic mission "in the light of reason."

Our data-informed approach to decision-making was shaped by my own experience leading institutional assessment processes in my previous work as an academic dean. My initial exposure to student learning assessment came from Barbara Walvoord's *Assessment Clear and Simple*, a resource I have used with faculty for nearly a decade. Her assessment model is both straightforward and effective. Walvoord encourages faculty to set clear goals, to gather meaningful data that can help assess these goals, and finally, to use this data to inform plans for improvements to student learning.

This assessment cycle is straightforward enough, but as most accreditors, higher education assessment directors, or academic deans will admit, data is often collected without setting clear and measurable goals from the outset, and there can often be cultural or institutional obstacles to articulating a clear path for assessment-driven improvement. This issue, so well described in William Myers's book *Closing the Assessment "Loop,"* leaves educators with piles of data but no obvious direction for implementation.

As with student learning assessment, our board began our discernment process with plenty of data in hand—much of it gathered through the work of the "Partners in Formation" research project. Though our goal might have been less clearly articulated than the student learning outcomes that we set for students on our syllabi, the board did have a shared sense that we needed the data to illuminate the viable options for the seminary's continued mission.

To close the loop, then, we needed a method that would help us to collectively engage with the data. We hoped for an approach that would prevent a single voice or interpretive position from eclipsing those of other members, that could lead us to identifying areas where further data was still needed, and that—most importantly—was open to the directing of the

Holy Spirit. In short, we needed a method of dealing with the data, in the words of Thomas Cranmer's collect for the second Sunday of Advent, that could help us "read, mark, and inwardly digest" the information that was in front of us.

I proposed a practice that I called "dwelling in the data," which was informed by a model of inductive Bible study popularized in Lutheran theologian Patrick Keifert's devotional text *Dwelling in the Word*. *Dwelling in the Word* has become a valuable resource for mainline congregations across the US that seek to foster a more meaningful engagement with Scripture. Both Keifert's "dwelling in the word" and my "dwelling in the data" involved communal engagement with the text (or the data), a willingness to be surprised or challenged by what the text (or the data) reveals, and a theologically grounded openness to what the Holy Spirit might illuminate in the process.[9]

When it came to our understanding of "reason" in the context of board discernment, dwelling in the data became an approach for the entire board to engage our collective God-given gift of reason. It prevented, from the outset, any single person claiming a privileged interpretive standpoint; it fostered a kind of epistemological humility that acknowledged that the data before us may challenge what we already know and, most importantly, may raise new questions about what we have yet to discover. Through "dwelling in the data," we were able to invite the active participation of God in our discernment by acknowledging that the human capacity for reason is itself grounded in divine gift.

All of this enabled our board to consider two key elements to the current challenge faced by the seminary: first, in terms of our programming, the seminary needed to develop a new and more accessible alternative to our master of divinity degree; second, because of the fragility of our operating model, we needed to either pursue a substantive combination with another institution, consider significantly downsizing our footprint on our current campus (leasing the majority to a third party), or cease instruction and become a fund that supported the educational activities of another institution.

In light of this, the next challenge would be to interpret these findings in light of a clear sense of the institution's tradition, that is, its ethos and historic mission.

---

9. Ellison and Keifert, *Dwelling in the Word*.

Tradition: Learning Our Story

> Some answer that to learn it we have no other way than only tradition; namely that so we believe because both we from our predecessors and they from theirs have so received.[10]

According to Richard Hooker, tradition plays a crucial role in the transmission of doctrine across generations. Particularly in terms of ecclesiology—the worship and governance of the church—tradition served to ensure continuity between the historic church and its contemporary manifestation. In his day, his approach to tradition contrasted with those of his Puritan rivals, who—steeped in the ethos of the Continental Reformation—feared that tradition was either non-scriptural or too Catholic.

In a similar way to how our board applied reason as we dwelled in the data in support of data-informed discernment, we employed tradition to "learn our story" and gain a clearer understanding of the mission, purpose, and identity of our institution over time. This was not a small task for a two-hundred-year-old seminary! To arrive at a clear understanding of our seminary's story, and thereby its historic mission, we employed three different research methodologies: historical research, survey research, and participant action research to help us "learn our story."

We consulted existing histories written about our institution, including Powel Dawley's comprehensive sesquicentennial book *The Story of General Seminary* (1967) and Edward Hardy's accessible article "The Organization and Early Years of the General Theological Seminary" (1936), the latter of which was reviewed by the entire board as part of a special board retreat. We read minutes of past board meetings, uncovered past accreditation reports, and combed through original copies of founding documents, including the seminary's charter with the state of New York and our original handwritten articles of incorporation. All of these documents helped us to gain a sense of the historic intention behind the founding of the institution, and gave us a clearer perspective of how the challenges that we faced in the moment related to similar challenges faced by our predecessors in the seminary's past.

Finally, since a majority of our board of trustees at the time were either alumni of the seminary or stakeholders within the church hierarchy, we dedicated considerable effort to listening to their collective experiences

---

10. Hooker, *Laws of Ecclesiastical Polity*, 1:3.8.14.

and memories of the institution. This form of participant action research resulted in what Clifford Geertz would have referred to as "thick descriptions" of our institution's mission and identity, all of which were grounded in concrete experiences of those associated with the institution's life.[11]

Through this work, we gained a clearer understanding of both General Seminary's ethos and its mission. In terms of the ethos, we read and heard stories about the important role played by outreach among our neighbors in New York City, supporting the idea that the urban context was a significant facet of the seminary's ethos. We heard and read further stories about the centrality of ascetical theology and the vibrant spiritual life that was promoted through regular eucharistic celebration and the regular practice of morning and evening prayer, all of which reflected the seminary's Benedictine ethos. Many alumni further reflected on the important role played by the seminary in introducing and preserving the Catholic tradition from within the American Episcopal Church, highlighting how the institution served as an important hub of liturgical and musical innovation in the twentieth century. Finally, both in terms of the seminary's historic curriculum and from the experience of recent graduates, we heard stories that emphasized the central role played by practical theology and field education in equipping our alumni for transformative ministry in a changing world.

By gaining a sense of our tradition, we identified who we were as an institution, enabling us to move forward with a clearer sense of purpose as we sought to live out our mission in a new way. With a clear awareness of ethos and mission, we arrived at two outcomes: a sense of the kind of partnership we wanted to pursue (one with another institution that similarly prepared individuals for ordained ministry in the Episcopal Church) and a sense of shared community and purpose as a board, which was necessary for the challenging work ahead.

Scripture: God's Transforming Work

> The Scripture of God is a storehouse abounding with inestimable treasures of wisdom and knowledge in many kinds, over and above things in this one kind barely necessary.[12]

---

11. Geertz, *Interpretation of Cultures*, 310.
12. Hooker, *Laws of Ecclesiastical Polity*, 1:3.9.16.

While I would like to think that Scripture informed our entire discernment process, there was a particular moment for me when Scripture most clearly entered the conversation. It was February of 2022, and I had been working on the agenda for our regular winter trustees' meeting. This was a pivotal moment preceded by months of "dwelling in the data" and the breakthrough during the January board retreat where we most clearly "learned our story." All of this pointed us away from the historic model of General Seminary as a stand-alone residential theological seminary and toward a new form of mission fulfillment.

At this stage, our discernment reflected what Luther described in the "Heidelberg Disputation"—we had become "theologians of the cross" who could "call a thing what it actually is."[13] We acknowledged the reality of declining enrollment, the unsustainability of our operating model, and the historic mission that called us to focus more squarely on ordination training for the Episcopal Church. The options before us—seeking institutional partnership, reducing our footprint, or ceasing instruction to become a fund supporting theological education—presented a stark reality, mirroring the "Stockdale Paradox" from Jim Collins's *Good to Great*:

> You must maintain unwavering faith that you can and will prevail in the end, regardless of the difficulties, and at the same time, have the discipline to confront the most brutal facts of your current reality, whatever they might be.[14]

As I engaged with Luther's theology of the cross and its resonance with the Stockdale Paradox, the gravity of our situation crystallized. Unlike previous attempts to address systemic challenges, this was not a search for quick solutions. We were acknowledging that the path forward required relinquishment—an institutional death—yet holding onto hope for resurrection. And yet, where death and resurrection stand juxtaposed, Christians find the Paschal mystery—a recognition that all life ends, yet through God's power, resurrection brings forth new, transformed life. As Ronald Rolheiser writes, "We must trust God enough to believe that nothing worthwhile will ever be lost and that he makes all things new."[15]

---

13. Luther, "Heidelberg Disputation," §21.
14. James Collins, *Good to Great*, 83–85.
15. Rolheiser, "Paschal Mystery," para. 4.

SECTION 4: EVERYDAY THEOLOGY IN INSTITUTIONAL LIFE

At the February board meeting, I led our trustees through an active reflection on the Paschal mystery, shaped by the final days of Christ: Maundy Thursday, Good Friday, Holy Saturday, Easter Sunday, and the ascension.

We began by contemplating Maundy Thursday—the Last Supper. Drawing from Eucharistic Prayer C in the *Book of Common Prayer* ("On the night he was betrayed, he took bread"), I invited the trustees to reflect on the gifts General Seminary had bestowed upon them and the wider church. We shared stories of joy, transformation, and the relationships nurtured within the seminary's chapel, classrooms, and community. Next, we turned to Good Friday, acknowledging the institutional death we faced. I invited the trustees to name what was dying—the traditional model, the physical space, and the sense of identity tied to General Seminary's historic footprint. The room filled with reflections on loss, grief, and the end of a cherished era. Holy Saturday followed—a day of silence and uncertainty. I recounted our chapel's tradition of being closed to the public on Holy Saturday, symbolizing absence and ambiguity. The trustees sat with the weight of institutional silence, imagining a world without General Seminary and the emptiness such absence would bring. Though resurrection is God's work, I asked the trustees to envision Easter Sunday—not as a return to the past but as a hope for new life. What elements of the seminary's mission should rise from the ashes? They voiced dreams of renewed mission, community, and relevance, trusting that the seminary's core calling would endure, even if transformed. Finally, we concluded with the ascension, reflecting on the disciples' transition from Christ's earthly presence to the empowerment of the Spirit. We affirmed that the mission of God at General Seminary would continue, carried forward by those called to shape theological education in the years ahead.

Through this journey of reflection, we discerned not only the necessity of letting go but the promise of renewal. Scripture had led us to face the truth with honesty but also to embrace the hope of resurrection, trusting that God's transforming work was not yet complete.

GENERAL SEMINARY'S PATH FORWARD

The discernment process led General Seminary to adopt a hybrid master of divinity program and enter into an affiliation with Virginia Theological Seminary. These decisions reflect the seminary's commitment to accessibility, collaboration, and sustaining its historic mission. The hybrid MDiv program addressed the challenges of declining residential enrollment by offering a flexible and affordable alternative. This innovation allowed the seminary to reach a broader audience while maintaining its commitment to rigorous theological education. The affiliation with Virginia Theological Seminary represented a bold step toward sustainability and collaboration. By combining resources, the two institutions created a partnership that preserved General's identity while enhancing its ability to fulfill its mission. The affiliation also allowed for a creative reimagining of the seminary's campus, leveraging its historic location in Chelsea to support its educational goals.

BROADER IMPLICATIONS

The journey of General Seminary reflects a larger truth—leadership, whether institutional or personal, is deeply theological. Decisions grounded in the integration of reason, tradition, and Scripture provide a model not only for theological education but for leadership in diverse contexts. This approach transcends the boundaries of ecclesial governance, offering a pathway for organizations, communities, and individuals to navigate complexity with clarity and faithfulness. By engaging data (reason), honoring institutional identity (tradition), and anchoring the process in God's unfolding work (Scripture), leaders cultivate a capacity to balance innovation with continuity. This posture invites humility—acknowledging the limits of human knowledge—while fostering trust in the transformative presence of the Spirit.

General Seminary's story illustrates that theological reflection can extend into boardrooms, financial decisions, and campus planning. It underscores that even institutional crises can become moments of discernment, spaces where God's work of death and resurrection unfolds in unexpected ways. As leaders lean into the hard work of discernment, they participate in a lived theology—where faith, shaped by reason and tradition, intersects with the real world.

Ultimately, the seminary's renewal points to a broader reality: institutions, like individuals, are vessels of God's ongoing creative and redemptive work. The practices that sustained General's transformation—deep listening, communal reflection, and trust in God's unfolding future—hold relevance far beyond theological education. They remind us that faithful leadership is not about preserving structures but about nurturing life,

Section 4: Everyday Theology in Institutional Life

fostering new expressions of mission that respond to the shifting landscapes of our time. Whether navigating institutional change, community leadership, or personal growth, the integration of reason, tradition, and Scripture offers a path toward grounded and transformative leadership—an embodiment of the lived theology that shapes every corner of our lives.

Conclusion
The Ordinary Sacred

THROUGHOUT THIS BOOK, WE have journeyed through the landscapes of everyday life, seeking the traces of divine presence in places that often go unnoticed. From the rhythms of popular culture to the challenges of institutional leadership, from the practices of making and creating to the complexities of environmental stewardship, we have sought to discern what it means to live a theology that is embedded in the quotidian. As we conclude, it is worth revisiting where we began: with the question of whether faith truly transforms the way we live each day.

The answer, as we have explored together, is a resounding yes. Theology is not a distant, abstract discipline confined to academic settings or Sunday sermons. It is a lived and living pursuit, one that meets us in the questions we ask, the communities we inhabit, and the cultures we navigate. This book has been a reflection on how God's presence saturates all of life—not just the so-called sacred but also the seemingly secular. It is in this recognition that we find the extraordinary within the ordinary, the sacred within the mundane.

A THEOLOGY FOR EVERYDAY LIFE

One of the central convictions of this work is that theology must meet us where we are. This is why we explored frameworks like the method of correlation and cultural studies, which help bridge the gap between the questions of contemporary life and the enduring truths of Christian faith. Through these methods, we see that theology does not stand apart from the world but is always in dialogue with it—challenging, critiquing, and learning from the cultures and contexts in which we live.

Conclusion

The theological themes we have engaged—from the imago Dei to the incarnation, from eschatological hope to the practices of worship and making—demonstrate that theology is not merely a set of doctrines but a way of seeing and engaging the world. These themes remind us that the God we worship is not only the creator of galaxies but also the sustainer of the intricate details of life, present in every corner of creation. Whether in the beauty of art, the joys and struggles of relationships, or the questions raised by technological and cultural shifts, theology calls us to attune ourselves to the presence of a God who is always near.

IMPLICATIONS FOR PRACTICE

As we bring this journey to a close, it is worth considering how these reflections might shape the way we live. First, this book invites us to cultivate attentiveness. The God we seek is often found in the interruptions, the small moments, and the spaces we might otherwise overlook. Attentiveness is a spiritual practice, one that opens our eyes to the ways God is at work in and through the world around us.

Second, it challenges us to embrace humility. A lived theology of everyday life recognizes that we do not have all the answers. Instead, we approach the world with a posture of curiosity and wonder, open to being surprised by grace. This humility also compels us to listen deeply—to the voices of others, to the needs of creation, and to the Spirit's quiet guidance.

Finally, it calls us to action. Theology is not simply about understanding; it is about transformation. Whether it is through acts of justice, practices of care, or the creative expressions of our gifts, theology invites us to participate in God's redemptive work in the world. This participation is not limited to grand gestures but is woven into the fabric of everyday decisions and relationships.

LOOKING FORWARD

As we move forward, let us carry with us the conviction that the ordinary is infused with the sacred. Let us seek God not only in moments of worship but also in the routines of work, play, and rest. Let us find hope in the promise that God is making all things new—even in the midst of our brokenness and doubt.

Conclusion

This is the invitation of a lived theology of everyday life: to see the world not as a distraction from faith but as a location of grace. It is an invitation to live with open hands and open hearts, ready to encounter the God who meets us in the most unexpected places. It is an invitation to live with love—for God, for neighbor, and for the world that God so loves.

CLOSING REFLECTION

As I reflect on this journey, I am reminded of the words of St. Augustine: "Thou hast formed us for Thyself, and our hearts are restless till they find rest in Thee."[1] This restlessness is not a burden but a gift—a reminder that we are always being drawn deeper into the mystery of God's love. In the end, this is what a lived theology is about: learning to love and be loved by the God who is with us in every moment.

May we go forth with eyes to see and hearts to respond, living each day as an act of worship and a testament to the God who makes all things new.

---

1. Augustine, *Confessions*, 45.

Bibliography

Anglican Communion. "Marks of Mission." Anglican Communion, n.d. https://www.anglicancommunion.org/mission/marks-of-mission.
Antal, Jim. *Climate Church, Climate World: How People of Faith Must Work for Change.* Lanham, MD: Rowman & Littlefield, 2023.
Archbishop's Council. *For Such a Time as This: A Renewed Diaconate in the Church of England; A Report to the General Synod of the Church of England of a Working Party of the House of Bishops.* General Synod Papers. London: Church, 2001.
Arnold, Matthew. *Culture and Anarchy.* Oxford World's Classics. New York: Oxford University Press, 1995.
Atkinson, David. *Renewing the Face of the Earth: A Theological and Pastoral Response to Climate Change.* London: SCM, 2008.
Attfield, Robert. *The Ethics of Environmental Concern.* London: Blackwell, 1983.
Augustine, Saint. *The Confessions of St. Augustin.* Edited by Philip Schaff. Translated by J. G. Pilkington. Vol. 1 of *The Nicene and Post-Nicene Fathers*, 1st ser. New York: Christian Literature, 1886.
Balthasar, Hans Urs von. *Seeing the Form.* Edited by Joseph Fessio and John Riches. Translated by Erasmo Leiva-Merikakis. Vol. 1 of *The Glory of the Lord: A Theological Aesthetics.* San Francisco: Ignatius, 1982.
Barbour, Ian G. *Technology, Environment, and Human Values.* New York: Praeger, 1980.
Barnett, James Monroe. *Diaconate: A Full and Equal Order.* Harrisburg, PA: Trinity, 1979.
Barthes, Roland. *Mythologies.* Translated by Annette Lavers. London: Vintage Classics, 2009.
Batdorf, Emily. "Living Paycheck to Paycheck Statistics 2024." *Forbes*, Apr. 2, 2024. https://www.forbes.com/advisor/banking/living-paycheck-to-paycheck-statistics-2024/.
Baudrillard, Jean. *Simulacra and Simulation.* Translated by Sheila Faria Glaser. Los Angeles: Semitext(e), 1981.
Beaudoin, Tom. *Witness to Dispossession: The Vocation of a Postmodern Theologian.* Maryknoll, NY: Orbis, 2008.

Bibliography

Begbie, Jeremy S. *Resounding Truth: Christian Wisdom in the World of Music*. Grand Rapids: Baker Academic, 2007.

———. *Voicing Creation's Praise: Towards a Theology of the Arts*. London: T&T Clark, 1991.

Berry, R. J. *God's Book of Works: The Nature and Theology of Nature*. London: T&T Clark, 2003.

Berryman, Jerome. *Godly Play: An Imaginative Approach to Religious Education*. Minneapolis: Fortress, 1995.

Bevans, Stephen B. *Models of Contextual Theology*. Rev. ed. Faith and Cultures. Maryknoll, NY: Orbis, 2002.

Bevans, Stephen B., and Roger P. Schroeder. *Prophetic Dialogue: Reflections on Christian Mission Today*. Maryknoll, NY: Orbis, 2011.

Black, Jeremy, et al., eds. *The Literature of Ancient Sumer*. Oxford: Oxford University Press, 2006.

Black, John N. *The Dominion of Man: The Search for Ecological Responsibility*. Edinburgh: Edinburgh University Press, 1970.

Bosch, David J. *Transforming Mission: Paradigm Shifts in the Theology of Mission*. American Society of Missiology. Maryknoll, NY: Orbis, 2001.

Bouma-Prediger, Steven. *For the Beauty of the Earth: A Christian Vision for Creation Care*. Engaging Culture. Grand Rapids: Baker Academic, 2001.

Brodd, Sven-Erik. "*Caritas* and *Diakonia* as Perspectives on the Diaconate." In *Ecclesiological Reflections*, edited by Gunnel Borgegård et al., 42–43. Vol. 2 of *The Ministry of the Deacon*. Uppsala: Nordic Ecumenical Council, 2000.

Brown, Frank Burch. *Good Taste, Bad Taste, and Christian Taste: Aesthetics in Religious Life*. Oxford: Oxford University Press, 2000.

Capps, Donald, and Nathan Carlin. "Releasing Life's Potential: A Pastoral Theology of Work." *Pastoral Psychology* 65 (2016) 863–83. http://dx.doi.org/10.1007/s11089-015-0674-0.

Case, Carl Delos. *The Masculine in Religion*. New York: American Baptist, 1906.

Cavalletti, Sofia. *The Religious Potential of the Child: Experiencing Scripture and Liturgy with Young Children*. 3rd ed. Chicago: Liturgy Training, 2020.

Certeau, Michel de. *The Practice of Everyday Life*. Translated by Steven Randall. Berkeley: University of California Press, 2002.

Chandler, Timothy, and Tara Magdalinski, eds. *With God on Their Side: Sport in the Service of Religion*. London: Routledge, 2002.

Chapman, Mark D. *Anglicanism: A Very Short Introduction*. Very Short Introductions. Oxford: Oxford University Press, 2006.

Chidester, David. *Authentic Fakes: Religion and American Popular Culture*. Oakland: University of California Press, 2005.

Clark, Lynn Schofield. *From Angels to Aliens: Teenagers, the Media, and the Supernatural*. Oxford: Oxford University Press, 2003.

Cole, Jonathan, and Peter Walker. *Theology on a Defiant Earth: Seeking Hope in the Anthropocene*. Religious Ethics and Environmental Challenges. Lanham, MD: Lexington, 2022.

Collins, James C. *Good to Great: Why Some Companies Make the Leap . . . and Others Don't*. New York: Collins, 2009.

Collins, John N. *Diakonia: Reinterpreting the Ancient Sources*. Oxford: Oxford University Press, 2009.

Bibliography

———. *Diakonia Studies: Critical Issues in Ministry*. Oxford: Oxford University Press, 2014.

Connell, W. F. *The Educational Thought and Influence of Matthew Arnold*. International Library of Sociology. Abingdon, UK: Routledge, 1998.

Cosden, Darrell T. "Work and the New Creation." Edited by Gregorio Guitián and Ana Marta González. *Scripta Theologica* 54 (2022) 757–87. https://doi.org/10.15581/006.54.3.757-787.

Cox, Harvey Gallagher. *The Feast of Fools: A Theological Essay on Festivity and Fantasy*. Cambridge, MA: Harvard University Press, 1969.

Dawley, Powel Mills. *The Story of the General Theological Seminary: A Sesquicentennial History, 1817–1967*. Oxford: Oxford University Press, 1969.

Deane-Drummond, Celia. *Eco-Theology*. London: Darton, Longman and Todd, 2008.

———. *A Handbook in Theology and Ecology*. London: SCM, 1996.

DeBerg, Betty A. *Ungodly Women: Gender and the First Wave of American Fundamentalism*. Minneapolis: Fortress, 1990.

DeLashmutt, Michael W. "Church and Climate Change: An Examination of the Attitudes and Practices of Cornish Anglican Churches Regarding the Environment." *Journal for the Study of Religion, Nature and Culture* 5 (2011) 61–81.

Doran, Robert M. *Theology and the Dialectics of History*. Heritage. Toronto: University of Toronto Press, 1990.

Durkheim, Émile. *The Elementary Forms of Religious Life*. Translated by Joseph Ward Swain. London: Allen & Unwin, 1915.

Dyrness, William A. *Poetic Theology: God and the Poetics of Everyday Life*. Grand Rapids: Eerdmans, 2011.

———. *Visual Faith: Art, Theology, and Worship in Dialogue*. Grand Rapids: Baker Academic, 2001.

Eco, Umberto. *The Role of the Reader: Explorations in the Semiotics of Texts*. Bloomington: Indiana University Press, 1979.

Ellison, Pat Taylor, and Patrick Keifert. *Dwelling in the Word*. Robbinsdale, MN: Church Innovations Institute, 2011.

ENS Staff. "General Seminary Strikes Pact with Real-Estate Developer." Archives of the Episcopal Church, Nov. 30, 2010. Press release 113010-04. https://episcopalarchives.org/cgi-bin/ENS/ENSpress_release.pl?pr_number=113010-04.

Episcopal Church. *The Book of Common Prayer, According to the Use of the Protestant Episcopal Church in the United States of America*. 2nd ed. New York: Whittaker, 1875.

Forbes, Bruce David, and Jeffrey H. Mahan, eds. *Religion and Popular Culture in America*. 3rd edition. Oakland: University of California Press, 2017.

Ford, David F., et al., eds. *The Modern Theologians: An Introduction to Christian Theology Since 1918*. 4th ed. Hoboken, NJ: Wiley-Blackwell, 2024.

Frampton, Andrew Marcus, et al. "Breakeven." Lyricfind, 2008. https://lyrics.lyricfind.com/lyrics/the-script-breakeven.

Freud, Sigmund. "Delusion and Dream: An Interpretation in the Light of Psychoanalysis of *Gradiva*, a Novel, by Wilhelm Jensen." Project Gutenberg, 1922. Translated by Helen M. Downey. Ebook 44917. https://www.gutenberg.org/files/44917/44917-h/44917-h.htm.

Gadamer, Hans-Georg. *Truth and Method*. Translated by Joel Weinsheimer and Donald G. Marshall. 2nd ed. London: Continuum Impacts, 2011.

Bibliography

Gallup. *State of the Global Workplace: The Voice of the World's Employees; Research Summary*. Washington, DC: Gallup, 2024. https://www.ahtd.org/files/state-of-the-global-workplace-2024-key-insights.pdf.
Garnham, Neal. "Both Praying and Playing: 'Muscular Christianity' and the YMCA in North-East County Durham." *Journal of Social History* 35 (2001) 397–407.
Geertz, Clifford. *The Interpretation of Cultures: Selected Essays*. New York: Basic, 1973.
Goldingay, John. *Exodus and Leviticus for Everyone*. Old Testament for Everyone. Louisville: Westminster John Knox, 2010.
Gooley, Anthony. "Deacons and the Servant Myth." *Pastoral Review* 2 (2006) 3–7.
Graham, Billy. "Are Sports Good for the Soul?" *Newsweek* (Jan. 11, 1971) 51–52.
Graham, Elaine, et al. *Theological Reflection: Methods*. London: SCM, 2005.
Green, Bernard. *Christianity in Rome: The First Three Centuries*. London: T&T Clark, 2010.
Green, Garrett. *Imagining God: Theology and the Religious Imagination*. San Francisco: Harper & Row, 1989.
Haight, Roger. *Dynamics of Theology*. Maryknoll, NY: Orbis, 2001.
Hardy, Edward Rochie. "The Organization and Early Years of the General Theological Seminary." *Historical Magazine of the Protestant Episcopal Church* 5 (1936) 147–76.
Heidegger, Martin. "The Question Concerning Technology." In *Basic Writings: From "Being and Time" (1927) to "The Task of Thinking" (1964)*, edited by David Farrell Krell, 320–29. New York: Harper Perennial Modern Thought, 2008.
Heifetz, Ronald A. *Leadership Without Easy Answers*. Cambridge, MA: Harvard University Press, 1998.
Hoffman, Shirl J., ed. *Sport and Religion*. Champaign, IL: Human Kinetics, 1992.
———. "Toward Narrowing the Gulf Between Sport and Religion." *WW* 33 (2003) 303–11.
Hooker, Richard. *Of the Laws of Ecclesiastical Polity*. Edited by R. W. Church. 2 vols. London: Penguin, 1984.
Hughes, Krista E., et al., eds. *Ecological Solidarities: Mobilizing Faith and Justice for an Entangled World*. World Christianity. Pennsylvania State University Press, 2019.
Huizinga, Johan. *Homo Ludens: A Study of the Play-Element in Culture*. Kettering, OH: Angelico, 2016.
Jenkins, Willis. *Ecologies of Grace: Environmental Ethics and Christian Theology*. Oxford: Oxford University Press, 2008.
Jensen, Robin M. *The Substance of Things Seen: Art, Faith, and the Christian Community*. Grand Rapids: Eerdmans, 2004.
John Paul II. "*Redemptoris Missio*: On the Permanent Validity of the Church's Missionary Mandate." Vatican, Dec. 7, 1990. https://www.vatican.va/content/john-paul-ii/en/encyclicals/documents/hf_jp-ii_enc_07121990_redemptoris-missio.html.
Joranko, Daniel. "Engaging the Climate Crisis Through Spiritual Nonviolence." In *Liberating People, Planet, and Religion: Intersections of Ecology, Economics, and Christianity*, edited by Joerg Rieger and Terra Schwerin Rowe, 211–33. Religion in the Modern World. Lanham, MD: Rowman & Littlefield, 2024.
Jorgenson, Kiara A., and Alan G. Padgett, eds. *Ecotheology: A Christian Conversation*. Grand Rapids: Eerdmans, 2020.
Kearns, Laurel. "Saving the Creation: Christian Environmentalism in the United States." *Sociology of Religion* 57 (1996) 55–70. https://doi.org/10.2307/3712004.
Leavis, Q. D. *Fiction and the Reading Public*. London: Chatto & Windus, 1932.

Bibliography

Lévi-Strauss, Claude. *Structural Anthropology.* New York: Basic, 1963.
Luther, Martin. "Heidelberg Disputation (1518)." Book of Concord, n.d. https://thebookofconcord.org/sources-and-context/heidelberg-disputation/.
Lynch, Gordon. *Understanding Theology and Popular Culture.* Hoboken, NJ: Wiley-Blackwell, 2004.
MacCulloch, Diarmaid. *Groundwork of Christian History.* London: Epworth, 1989.
Marcuse, Herbert. *One-Dimensional Man: Studies in the Ideology of Advanced Industrial Society.* Routledge Classics. Abingdon, UK: Routledge & Kegan Paul, 1964.
Marlow, Hilary, and Mark Harris, eds. *The Oxford Handbook of the Bible and Ecology.* Oxford Handbooks. Oxford: Oxford University Press, 2022.
McFague, Sallie. *The Body of God: An Ecological Theology.* London: SCM, 1993.
McLean, Jeanne P. *Leading from the Center: The Emerging Role of the Chief Academic Officer in Theological Schools.* Durham, NC: Duke University Press, 1999.
McRobbie, Angela. *Postmodernism and Popular Culture.* Abingdon, UK: Routledge, 1994.
mohaupt, abby. "Corporate Confession, The Presbyterian Church (USA), and Fossil Fuels." In *Liberating People, Planet, and Religion: Intersections of Ecology, Economics, and Christianity,* edited by Joerg Rieger and Terra Schwerin Rowe, 193–210. Religion in the Modern World. Lanham, MD: Rowman & Littlefield, 2024.
Moltmann, Jürgen. *God in Creation: An Ecological Doctrine of Creation.* Translated by Margaret Kohl. Gifford Lectures 1984–85. London: SCM, 1985.
Moltmann, Jürgen, et al. *Theology of Play.* New York: Harper & Row, 1972.
Morgan, David. *The Forge of Vision: A Visual History of Modern Christianity.* Berkeley: University of California Press, 2015.
———. *Visual Piety: A History and Theory of Popular Religious Images.* Berkeley: University of California Press, 1998.
Mulvey, Laura. *Visual Pleasure and Narrative Cinema.* Edited by Mark Lewis. Artwork by Rachel Rose. Afterall Books: Two Works. London: Afterall, 2016.
Myers, William. *Closing the Assessment "Loop": Nurturing Healthy On-Going Self-Evaluation in Theological Schools.* New York: Exploration, 2006.
Nash, Jennifer. "Multiple Jobholders Account for 5.3% of Workers in June 2025." Advisor Perspectives, July 7, 2025. https://www.advisorperspectives.com/dshort/updates/2025/07/07/multiple-jobholders-account-for-5-3-of-workers-in-june-2025.
Niebuhr, H. Richard. *Christ and Culture.* New York: Harper Brothers, 1950.
Nordstokke, Kjell, ed. "*Diakonia* in Context: Transformation, Reconciliation, Empowerment." Lutheran World Federation, Jan. 2009. https://lutheranworld.org/resources/document-diakonia-context-transformation-reconciliation-empowerment.
Northcott, Michael S. *God and Gaia: Science, Religion and Ethics on a Living Planet.* Routledge Environmental Humanities. London: Routledge, Taylor & Francis, 2023.
———. "Ecology and Christian Ethics." In *The Cambridge Companion to Christian Ethics,* edited by Robin Gill, 209–27. Cambridge Companions to Religion. Cambridge: Cambridge University Press, 2000.
———. *The Environment and Christian Ethics.* New Studies in Christian Ethics 10. Cambridge: Cambridge University Press, 1996.
Nottingham, Elizabeth K. *Religion and Society.* New York: Random House, 1954.

Bibliography

Otterman, Sharon. "Seeking Dean's Firing, Seminary Professors End Up Jobless." *New York Times*, Oct. 1, 2014. https://www.nytimes.com/2014/10/02/nyregion/labor-dispute-leaves-professors-jobless.html.

Pals, Daniel L. *Seven Theories of Religion*. Oxford: Oxford University Press, 1996.

Parker, Rozsika. *The Subversive Stitch: Embroidery and the Making of the Feminine*. London: Women's, 1984.

Paul VI. "*Evangelii Nuntiandi*: Apostolic Exhortation." Vatican, Dec. 8, 1975. https://www.vatican.va/content/paul-vi/en/apost_exhortations/documents/hf_p-vi_exh_19751208_evangelii-nuntiandi.html.

Piercy, Marge. "To Be of Use." In *Circles on the Water: Selected Poems of Marge Piercy*, 106. New York: Knopf, 1982.

Plate, S. Brent. *Religion, Art, and Visual Culture: A Cross-Cultural Reader*. London: Palgrave, 2002.

———. *Walter Benjamin, Religion, and Aesthetics: Rethinking Religion Through the Arts*. Abingdon, UK: Routledge, 2005.

Posadas, Jeremy D. "The Refusal of Work in Christian Ethics and Theology: Interpreting Work from an Anti-Work Perspective." *Journal of Religious Ethics* 45 (2017) 330–61.

Prebish, Charles S. *Religion and Sport: The Meeting of Sacred and Profane*. Contributions to the Study of Popular Culture 36. Westport, CT: Greenwood, 1993.

Putney, Clifford. *Muscular Christianity: Manhood and Sports in Protestant America, 1880–1920*. Cambridge, MA: Harvard University Press, 2001.

Quinsey, Katherine M. *Christian Environmentalism and Human Responsibility in the 21st Century: Questions of Stewardship and Accountability*. Routledge Explorations in Environmental Studies. London: Routledge, 2024.

Rahner, Hugo. *Man at Play*. New York: Herder & Herder, 1972.

Richmann, Christopher J. "What Are They Saying (and Not Saying) About Vocation?" *WW* 43 (2023) 199–207.

Ricoeur, Paul. *Freud and Philosophy: An Essay on Interpretation*. Translated by Denis Savage. 11th ed. Terry Lectures. New Haven, CT: Yale University Press, 1977.

Rolheiser, Ron. "Paschal Mystery: The New You." Ron Rolheiser, OMI, June 3, 1985. https://ronrolheiser.com/paschal-mystery-the-new-you/.

Sanders, T. C. Review of *Two Years Ago*, by Charles Kingsley. *Saturday Review* 3 (Feb. 21, 1857) 176–77.

Sarto, Pablo Blanco. "El trabajo en Martín Lutero y autores luteranos recientes." *Scripta Theologica* 55 (2023) 271–96. https://doi.org/10.15581/006.55.2.271-296.

Schillebeeckx, Edward. *God the Future of Man*. Translated by N. D. Smith. Theological Soundings 5.1. London: Sheed and Ward, 1969.

Southgate, Christopher, ed. *God, Humanity and the Cosmos: A Companion to the Science-Religion Debate*. 2nd ed. Edinburgh: T&T Clark, 2010.

Spencer, Nick, and Robert White. *Christianity, Climate Change and Sustainable Living*. London: SPCK, 2007.

Stone, Allister. "John Calvin, the Work Ethic, and Vocation." *Western Reformed Seminary Journal* 16 (2009) 24–30.

Storey, John. *An Introduction to Cultural Theory and Popular Culture*. Harlow, UK: Longman, 1997.

Sykes, Stephen. *The Study of Anglicanism*. London: SPCK, 1998.

Tanner, Kathryn. *Theories of Culture: A New Agenda for Theology*. Guides to Theological Inquiry. Minneapolis: Fortress, 1997.

Bibliography

Taylor, Charles. *A Secular Age*. Cambridge, MA: Belknap, 2018.

Tertullian. "The Shows, or *De Spectaculis*." Translated by S. Thelwall. In *The Ante-Nicene Fathers*, edited by Alexander Roberts et al., 3:79–92. Buffalo, NY: Christian Literature, 1885.

Theology of Work Project, Inc. "Calling in the Theology of Work." *Journal of Markets & Morality* 14 (2011) 171–87.

Thiselton, Anthony. *The First Epistle to the Corinthians: A Commentary on the Greek Text*. NIGTC. Grand Rapids: Eerdmans, 2000.

Tillich, Paul. *Systematic Theology*. 3 vols. Chicago: University of Chicago Press, 1967.

———. *Theology of Culture*. Edited by Robert C. Kimball. New York: Oxford University Press, 1959.

Tracy, David. *Blessed Rage for Order: The New Pluralism in Theology*. New York: Seabury, 1975.

Van Montfoort, Trees. *Green Theology: An Eco-Feminist and Ecumenical Perspective*. London: Darton, Longman and Todd, 2022.

Vaughn, J. Patrick. "The Sanctuary as Playground: A Metaphor for Our Experience of Worship." *QR* 16 (1996) 57–71.

Vaughn, Kassandra. "You Will Spend 90,000 Hours of Your Lifetime at Work: Are You Happy?" Medium, May 5, 2018. https://kassandravaughn.medium.com/you-will-spend-90-000-hours-of-your-lifetime-at-work-are-you-happy-5a2b5b0120ff.

Volf, Miroslav. "Work as Cooperation with God." In *Work: Theological Foundations and Practical Implications*, edited by R. Keith Loftin and Trey Dimsdale, 83–109. London: SCM, 2018.

Walvoord, Barbara E. Fassler. *Assessment Clear and Simple: A Practical Guide for Institutions, Departments, and General Education*. Jossey-Bass Higher Education. Hoboken, NJ: Jossey-Bass, 2010.

Ward, Graham. *Cities of God*. Radical Orthodoxy. London: Routledge, 2002.

———. *Cultural Transformation and Religious Practice*. Cambridge: Cambridge University Press, 2005.

———. *Politics of Discipleship: Becoming Postmaterial Citizens*. Grand Rapids: Baker Academic, 2009.

———. *True Religion*. Wiley-Blackwell Manifestos. Malden, MA: Blackwell, 2003.

Westermann, Claus. *Genesis 1–11: A Commentary*. London: SPCK, 1984.

White, Lynn, Jr. "The Historical Roots of Our Ecological Crisis." *Science*, n.s., 155 (1967) 1203–7.

Williams, Jack. "Playing Church: Understanding Ritual and Religious Experience Resourced by Gadamer's Concept of Play." *International Journal of Philosophy and Theology* 79 (2018) 323–36. https://doi.org/10.1080/21692327.2017.1406817.

Williams, Raymond. *Keywords: A Vocabulary of Culture and Society*. New York: Oxford University Press, 1983.

———. *Resources of Hope: Culture, Democracy, Socialism*. London: Verso, 1989.

Winnicott, Donald W. *Playing and Reality*. Routledge Classics. London: Routledge, 1997.

Yanagi, Soetsu. *The Beauty of Everyday Things*. Translated by Michael Brase. Penguin Modern Classics. London: Penguin, 2018.

Žižek, Slavoj, dir. *The Pervert's Guide to Cinema*. Vienna: Mischief, 2006.

www.ingramcontent.com/pod-product-compliance
Lightning Source LLC
Chambersburg PA
CBHW022114160426
43197CB00009B/1022